The Gift Is Already Yours

The Gift Is Already Yours

Erwin E. Prange

Bethany Fellowship INC.
MINNEAPOLIS, MINNESOTA 55438

REV. ERWIN E. PRANGE is associate pastor of a large Lutheran church as well as associate pastoral counselor at the Center for Christian Psychotherapy in Roseville, Minnesota. He has authored other books, including *How to Pray for Your Children* and *A Time for Intercession*, and numerous articles for church publications.

The Gift Is Already Yours
Erwin E. Prange

Library of Congress Catalog Card Number 79-55545

ISBN 0-87123-189-1

Published by Bethany Fellowship, Inc.
6820 Auto Club Road, Minneapolis, Minnesota 55438

Printed in the United States of America

FOREWORD

"My Prussian ancestors," says the author, "had bred into me a deep distrust of the emotions." And Lutherans have a tendency to equate "emotion" with "experience." So Erwin Prange was no pushover for some contrived religious experience. *Reality* is what he sought. And reality is what he found—

In the quiet sanctuary of an inner-city church in Brooklyn, where he experienced in a new way the reality of the Holy Spirit . . .

In New York hospital rooms, where God manifested his healing power . . .

In the sub-basement of a theological library, where the story of a Lutheran charismatic from another century set his soul on fire . . .

In the riot-torn streets of the City, where God showed his peace in the midst of violence . . .

In the call of God to become a bridge of reconciliation between two congregations, one white, one black . . .

This story of a Lutheran pastor's quest for a more meaningful life and ministry begins where many people begin—with a vague sense of dissatisfaction with everyday religious routine. Then he reached out for more, and found that God had more to give! The realities of the Bible began to be reenacted in the tough world of the inner-city—healings, conversions, peace-in-the-midst-of-persecution, deliverance, exorcisms.

This book has a certain feeling of *stability* about it, a sense of roots, of history; an appreciation of one's tradition and heritage, even as it moves out on the frontier of what God is doing in our own day. (The author's "discovery" of Pastor Johann Christoph Blumhardt, a Lutheran charismatic of the 19th Century, is one of the most exciting chapters in the book.)

The author's approach to the charismatic dimension of Christian experience will be especially meaningful for those who come from a "sacramental" tradition—Catholic, Lutheran, Anglican, Orthodox. He demonstrates that the vitality of the charismatic experience is not limited to a denomination or a particular theological formula—it is a dynamic movement of God which no theological analysis can fully exhaust, yet which enriches one's most cherished traditions and beliefs.

Larry Christenson

PREFACE

It has been over fifteen years since that memorable day, December 7, 1963, when God became real for me. There has been much joy as well as pain. Both were necessary for growth. I have been constantly reminded of my baptismal covenant, "Receive the sign of the holy cross both upon the forehead and upon the breast in token that thou shalt henceforth know the fellowship of the Lord's sufferings and the power of His resurrection."

I went the long way, round about by way of the wilderness. This book is written for my fellow pilgrims in the hope that they might profit from my mistakes and also know that they are not alone.

If there are hungry hearts anywhere searching for more of God, may they know that there is more—infinitely more, right in their own churches. The Word can become flesh in your own life.

The Spirit comes in many different ways to different people (I Cor. 12). God manifests Himself to us according to our individual needs and personalities. Yet He comes to us also in the context of the church with all of its human and divine aspects. His gifts are always, first and foremost, gifts to the Body rather than to the individual.

This is a book written by a Lutheran from a Lutheran perspective. I humbly pray that it might also be a living letter written by the Holy Spirit to be opened and read by all men. It is a letter about Jesus Christ written on the quivering flesh of my own heart. Sometimes the writing is blurred and the words scrawled because the ghostly finger of the Spirit used the kind of material I am. With the bloody pen of the cross, He wrote deep down inside me where all my willing and doing originate. For this reason, the book is personal and intimate. There was a long time during which I wondered whether I should share it at all.

Erwin Prange

CONTENTS

I

BROOKLYN

It was the summer of '63—the first long, hot, city summer for my family. In the Brooklyn ghetto, where as many as one hundred thousand people were squeezed into one square mile, the air crackled with tension. The city was a pressure cooker threatening to explode. Like the advance shocks of an earthquake, the first signs of the great ghetto riots to come—Brooklyn, Chicago, Watts—were breaking through.

As I walked up Jefferson Street from Bushwick Avenue, the spilling-over garbage cans greeted me like old friends. Except for the huge old pear tree in the backyard of St. Mark's parsonage, there was hardly a spot of green to break the monotony of cement, asphalt, and steel. "Old friends," I thought, "you're not beautiful, but you are useful. Only why do you have to be emptied at 2:00 A.M.—and banged on the sidewalk after being dumped into the grinder?" It was all a part of the city symphony, a symphony which never ended.

I remembered the little river town in Arkansas where I was born in 1917. The road ended in Crockett's Bluff, and there wasn't even a train. I was eleven when I saw my first train: the locomotive suddenly blew off steam and whistled, and I clapped my hands over my ears and ran in terror. I remembered the dry, clear air in West Texas where we moved when I was eleven. The cool nights were heavy with silence, and you could almost reach out and touch the stars.

What was Tom Sawyer, turned Texan, doing in the midst of all this din? In 1948, when I came back from Europe after spending almost five years overseas with the Army, I had passed through Brooklyn. It was a harrowing experience. The Brooklyn streets had seemed more dangerous than the foxholes of World War II. I remembered saying, "I don't know what I'm going to do or where I'm going, but I will never, never, live in Brooklyn!" What was I doing here now? Did the Lord send me? I didn't know Him personally when I came, but years later He would tell me what had happened could have happened only in Brooklyn.

Jefferson Street began at the intersection of Broadway and Myrtle, just half a block from St. Mark's huge nineteen-room parsonage. At Broadway and Myrtle, two elevated trains crossed each other above the busy street traffic. Every working day, a number of people equal to the populations of seven western states passed that way. They were black, white, brown, yellow, and red—plus all the shades in between. They spoke fifty different languages and came from a hundred different countries. What had brought them all together into this one hot, crowded place?

The Chemical and Lincoln Banks on the opposite sides of Broadway were a symbol of the answer. Money and the dream of success had attracted these millions to New York. They had come from all over the United States and the whole world. Less than one percent had really made it. The money buried in the deep vaults of the banks almost seemed to mock the poverty of the millions who passed over it every day.

A drugstore, a liquor store, and an army surplus store bracketed the rest of the Broadway-Myrtle-Jefferson corner. Around the fringes were a few neat little shops left over from the days when Williamsburg was a thriving German-American community. A newsstand and the liquor store served as anchor points for the Elevated entrances and exits. John & Al's Sporting Goods Store was in the middle of the block. Years later it was to become famous when four men used its guns and ammunition to hold off the New York City police for over two days.

I was in the habit of dropping in to chat with Mel at the liquor store whenever I needed communion wine, Scotch, or just happened to be passing by. Mel was a Missouri Synod Lutheran with a deep spiritual hunger. He knew that there was something missing in his church life, but he also knew that if he joined a Fundamentalist church, he might have to find a new way of earning a living. Often we would share our frustrations and wonder why the Lord had dropped us off on this particular corner.

My clerical collar sometimes startled Mel's customers a bit, especially if they happened to be Baptist deacons. I felt a bit uncomfortable myself, even though Lutherans tended to be very permissive about alcohol.

"Hello, Father," an ex-altar boy said one afternoon.

"Hi, how are things going?"

"Okay I guess, Father. Maybe I should leave this stuff alone, but it helps me to forget for a while."

"What is it you are trying to forget?" I asked, putting on my best counseling manner.

5

"Well, I was an altar boy once and a good Catholic, but that was a long time ago, and a lot of things have happened since. But I still believe in God, and I know He does forgive. Say a prayer for me, Father." With that, he crossed himself, tipped his hat, and ordered a pint of Scotch. He had touched all bases.

Sometimes Mel's customers were already drunk, and he would refuse to sell them anything more to drink. They would argue and then begin to threaten. Many times, drunks would have to be escorted and even thrown out of the liquor store. "What a way to have to earn a living," I thought. "Being a ghetto pastor isn't as bad as that, even if you don't believe in what you're doing."

One day I followed a wino out into the street. He had managed to get by Mel's scrutiny and was fondling the pint of Sneaky Pete he had purchased with cadged quarters. Somewhat unsteadily, he found a seat under the steps of the El. He might have been fifty years old; he could easily have passed for seventy. With trembling hands, he tore the top off the bottle of cheap red wine and then let it flow like healing balm down his parched throat. What was bugging him so that mere consciousness was such a terrible burden? Was it guilt or fear or some terrible inner thirst that only alcohol could slake? I could remember having a pretty big beer thirst after I got out of the Army, but it was never like this. In one of my theological books, I had read that every hunger and thirst was really a hunger and thirst for God. It sounded so good that I had even preached about it several times. But what did it really mean? Did this wino really have a spiritual thirst? Was the strange longing that often gnawed at my own guts a spiritual hunger?

6

At that moment, the wino spotted me and tried to hide his bottle. He took off his cap and crossed himself.

"Father, could you spare a quarter for a cup of coffee?" It sounded like a reflex action.

"Coffee?" I asked, glancing at the half-hidden bottle.

"Well, Father, some people like coffee and some people like other things. I just happen to like wine, but I want you to know I'm not an alcoholic. I never hurt anybody, and I have faith in God. I respect the Church, and I respect you, Father. Now, how about that quarter?"

I reached into my pocket as I was to do thousands of times in New York, haunted by the words of Matthew 25: "I was thirsty, and you gave me no drink." I wondered what the Lord really meant by that one. Could it possibly include winos? Not long before, I had decided to play it safe and give no less than a dollar to everyone who asked me, a decision that was to cost me more than five thousand dollars before I left New York.

The old derelict, the grimy buildings, and the run-down stores all spoke of better and happier days. I could close my eyes and almost see Williamsburg when it was still an all-German community. It must have been spotlessly clean and fairly bustling with Teutonic energy. One could almost hear the happy German gutturals floating out of the "Bierstuben." How things had changed! Now all you heard was clipped New Yorkese, rapid Spanish, and the soft slur of the South turned aggressive. But the biggest change wasn't in sight or sound. It was in attitude. The happy days were gone forever. The dream was dead. One could stand at the corner of Broadway and Myrtle all afternoon and not see a single smiling face. If you heard a happy voice on the train, you knew immediately that it belonged to a tourist, probably from the Midwest. Even on our block, neighbors seldom greeted one another. They sat with blank faces at the window or on the stoop, watching the many passersby and keeping their thoughts to themselves.

St. Mark's Church was an impressive reminder of the past. Its copper-sheathed, Gothic tower reached 219 feet into the Brooklyn sky, and the plant covered a whole block-front on once fashionable Bushwick Avenue, then known as "The Avenue of the Churches." The sanctuary seated some 1,400 people; its parochial school had once had a peak enrollment of 750 pupils; and until World War I, German was the primary language in church and school.

St. Mark's was indeed a city built on a hill—a giant, Gothic prayer pointing heavenward at the crossroads of the world. The crossroads may have become profane, but there was still something deeply holy about that cross-topped arm reaching up to praise God. St. Mark's was built long before World War I and the automobile scattered her expatriate German kingdom, but here she remained quietly blessing Brooklyn. Her builders would have frowned at much that now took place beneath her silent benediction, but perhaps God had designed her for just such a time as this. For as it brooded over the great ghettos of Bedford-Stuyvesant, Bushwick, and Williamsburg, the cross seemed to be saying, "God is watching; don't give up hope."

Bedford-Stuyvesant, at one time a very fashionable neighborhood, was now the Harlem of Brooklyn. Her brownstones were decaying, and her once busy synagogues and Hebrew schools stood almost empty. Locked into this largest black community in the world was most of the despair of the American Negro, and here, too, the fuse for the urban riots of the sixties was sputtering.

After World War II, Williamsburg became the home of the largest Hasidic Jewish community in the world. The Hasidim—with their beards, black hats, and long black coats, which they wore even in the hottest weather—were without doubt the most unmeltable group in New York's melting pot. I watched them on the trains reading their Torahs, Talmuds, and Yiddish newspapers. Yiddish, an old German dialect written in Hebrew letters, was the international language of world Jewry. Because I knew German and had studied Hebrew, I could read it, and sometimes when I wore my clerical collar on the subway, I would buy a Yiddish newspaper, just to see the consternation on the faces of blasé New Yorkers at the sight of what they took to be a Catholic priest reading a Jewish newspaper. I was intrigued with the Hasidim who had changed so little through the many centuries. Abraham, Isaac and Jacob, Isaiah and Jeremiah must have looked just like those bearded, black-robed figures. Our Lord Himself may have looked something like one of those gentle, mystic, young men.

Williamsburg was also becoming the Spanish Harlem of Brooklyn, and from the time that St. Mark's began to hold regular Spanish-language services in 1959, it ministered to a succession of transient Spanish congregations. Through the annexation of Puerto Rico by the United States, Puerto Ricans had automatically become American citizens. The great wave of Puerto Rican immigrants had been almost more than even New York could absorb. From the beginning, they flocked to New York City and settled in bleak, homogenous, ghetto communities. They had abandoned their lush, warm, island home and come to cold, dirty New York for one reason only—Yankee dollars.

Contrary to the "lazy Latin" stereotype, Puerto Ricans talk and work rapidly and seem to have a high degree of natural manual skill, and for this reason they were sought after by factories and service industries. However, most of them had been catapulted, almost overnight, from a simple country life into a crowded industrial and technical society. They simply couldn't cope with things like sanitation, time payments, and building codes. The tremendous, unalleviated tensions of city living too often led them into the escape-traps of drugs and then crime. Other immigrant groups had burned their bridges behind them when they came and had achieved American citizenship through considerable effort. The Puerto Ricans were given U.S. citizenship en masse, with or without English. They could always fly back to San Juan for thirty-eight dollars. This resulted in a kind of cultural schizophrenia. They lived with one foot in Puerto Rico and the other in New York and commuted back and forth with the times and tides of fortune.

Bushwick acted as a kind of buffer zone between black, white, and brown pockets of population and as such often found itself a battle zone as well. It still had an Italian enclave where the Schlitz and Rheingold breweries were located and where many old "Mafia" families were still reputed to be living. Sometimes older residents would whisper stories about a local bakery in whose huge ovens

Murder, Incorporated, was said to have disposed of its bodies.

One day someone on Central Avenue said, "Rev, don't believe all those stories about putting people in a barrel of concrete and dropping them in the East River. That's too much trouble, and concrete blocks are too hard to hide. Do you know how hot a bakery oven gets? Why, there aren't even any ashes left, no matter what you burn."

"But what about the police—and what about the bakery customers?"

"Forget the police, and as far as the customers go, that bakery still makes the best bread and cakes in the whole city."

I shuddered a little and reminded myself never to become one of those customers. Were they putting me on, or was Brooklyn really like that? From that time on, every time I drove past the bakery, I experienced a slightly queasy feeling in the pit of my stomach. The outraged ghosts of Murder, Incorporated, seemed to be shimmering in the heat above the bakery's chimney.

There was no question that the Mafia was real. One day I made the mistake of turning in a list of suspected drug pushers to the precinct. The next day, the doorbell rang, and I had a visitor. He was polite, soft-spoken, and well dressed. We stood outside and talked. Through the back gate, I could see our four children playing in the tiny backyard of the parsonage that was their whole outside world. I saw Margie framed in the kitchen window of the parsonage.

"Nice family you have there, Rev," my visitor said softly, taking them all in.

11

"Thank you. I like them too."

"Be too bad if something happened to them."

"Yes, it would be." Suddenly I was angry, and for one mad moment I thought of my old shotgun upstairs. Then I said, with far more confidence than I felt, "The Lord will take care of them." My visitor tipped his hat and left quickly.

One night I heard an unusual clattering among the garbage cans across the street, then the unmistakable moans of a mugging victim. I ran to the window and saw two dark figures running down the street, and a man lying in a dark pool in the middle of the sidewalk. I told Margie to call the police, grabbed my bathrobe, and ran downstairs and into the street. An elderly brewery worker, coming off the 2:30 A.M. shift, had been robbed and badly beaten. The police came, the ambulance came, and when the neighbors saw me out on the street, they ventured out of their apartments, gathering in little knots. I picked up snatches of conversation: "Isn't it terrible?" "Why don't the police do something?" "What's the world coming to?" "I can remember when this neighborhood was as safe as a church." Before long, the neighbors started yawning and went back to bed. Such assaults were happening twice a week just on our block.

Survival was one thing, ministry another. How did you form the Body of Christ out of people who didn't even notice or speak to each other? One day I went to call on a German family in a small, six-family apartment house in the Ridgewood section of Brooklyn. The name wasn't on the mailbox or the bell, but I knew that they lived somewhere

12

inside. I rang the bell of the front apartment on the first floor. "Pardon me, but I'm looking for the Schmidt family."

"Sorry, Father, never heard of them." The door closed quickly.

Eventually, I found Mrs. Schmidt in the rear apartment on the third floor. We spoke in German.

"Mrs. Schmidt, how long have you been living here?"

"Over twenty years, Pastor."

"The people in the first apartment downstairs, how long have they been here?"

"About eighteen years, I think."

"Do you know their name?"

"No."

"Do you ever pass in the hallway?"

"Yes."

"Do you ever speak?"

"No."

Coming from Texas, I simply could not believe it. But I soon learned just how hideously impersonal a big city can be. I heard stories about people being in chronic-care institutions for over thirty years without having a single visitor. A few years later, a young girl was stabbed to death over a period of forty-five minutes in front of thirty-eight witnesses who didn't even bother to call the police. The world was appalled; New Yorkers weren't even surprised.

It was a time of gangs and war in the streets. I encountered the gangs many times on my nightly rounds. They looked as if they were trying to blend into the dark street corners. The colors of their uniforms and the shapes of their skinny frames seemed to be almost painted on the drab surroundings. Only the low murmur of voices and short bursts of laughter indicated that the shadows were alive.

"Evening, Father."

"Good evening. Enjoying the cool night air?"

The murmur stopped. Then the menacing attitude relaxed, and I heard a few embarrassed giggles after I passed. I felt them staring silently after my retreating figure, black suit, white collar, white face. To them, I was the squarest of the squares.

How and where could we meet? Was there some halfway house where each could unmask a little? It was a long way from the wide-open, sunbaked plains of Texas to the battleground of Bedford-Stuyvesant where kids played their deadly games with knives and zip guns. Where did the church fit into this picture? The peaceful rural scenes on St. Mark's massive stained-glass windows were a million miles from this reality. They seemed to symbolize the church as a dying pastoral island in midst of a surging urban sea.

I had to do something. But where could I start? What did Jesus mean to me?

II

A MAN BORN OUT OF DUE SEASON

The summer of '63 had to be the hottest on record. The heat seemed to come up from the sidewalks in waves. In July, we were to leave on our yearly vacation. This time, packing was especially hectic, because I had gotten a family camping outfit from Sears and Roebuck.

Margie's enthusiasm was not exactly boundless. "Why did you have to spend all that money?" She shook her head. "And just where are we going camping? You've never been exactly the outdoor type, and the children are too young to help. Where are you going to put all this junk, anyhow?"

"On top of the wagon," I said lightly. "Five nights on the road, and we'll have saved the cost of it. Besides, think of all the fun it will be camping out under the stars after being cooped up for so long."

"Well, this I've got to see. I just can't picture you roughing it. There are a lot of other things out in nature besides stars."

Packing was invariably complicated by the fact that St. Mark's, for all its frontage, didn't have a single driveway. In 1890, people really hadn't taken the automobile too seri-

15

ously. In order to park our Chevie wagon, we had to "jay" park on narrow Jefferson Street and dodge trucks while tying down the load. Between loads, someone had to stay with the car to keep what had been brought out from being stolen. Usually the whole neighborhood watched, and we felt a little guilty about being able to escape even for a couple of weeks while the rest were condemned to stay and simmer.

Finally, everything was packed and tied down, the canvas ground cover neatly stretched over the roof rack. The little ones had been sent back inside to go to the bathroom one more time, and the twentieth trip had been made to retrieve some forgotten item.

When we finally escaped, we had to fight Manhattan and tunnel traffic for over an hour before reaching the Jersey Turnpike. How good it was to leave the city behind and to see green fields again! Miles later, as the fresh, clean air broke through, you could almost hear one lung saying to the other, "That's the stuff I've been telling you about." It was like being a boy again.

That night we drove straight through. The smell of new-mown hay along the Pennsylvania Turnpike was Chanel No. 5. The damp, cool air and the towering trees were healing balm for city-sick souls. The children and Margie slept, and as I drove through the long, silent night, I again wondered why I had ever gone to the city. Somehow God always seemed nearer in the woods and fields than He did in the concrete and steel canyons.

By the following evening, we were near St. Louis. I had

driven over a thousand miles. We collapsed in a Holiday Inn, with no thought of camping. But the long drive had purged the tension of Brooklyn, and we all slept like farmers.

The following day, we made it to the farm in Northeast Oklahoma where Margie's parents lived. Margie used to say that she came from Coffeyville, Kansas, where she went to high school, because she felt Kansas sounded more respectable than Oklahoma. I could understand; I had always felt a little embarrassed about being born in Arkansas. Not that New Yorkers cared one bit; as far as they were concerned, there was nothing but Indians and wilderness anywhere west of the Hudson. Some of them even seemed to feel that if you went very far west of the Mississippi, you stood a fair chance of falling off the edge of the world.

The 375-acre farm where Margie had grown up was a real change for children raised on Jefferson Street. Karen was two and Diane one when we moved to New York. Both boys had been born in Brooklyn. When Karen was seven and Diane six, they had traveled alone on the El to parochial school in Glendale, some eight miles from home. They had to change to a bus, and at rush hour encountered thousands of people in the Broadway-Myrtle Station. Mark had played stickball and dodged trucks in the streets when he was five. Trains, trucks, and street gangs didn't faze them, but strange insects could put them beside themselves. Occasionally, during our Oklahoma visit, we would hear a piercing shriek from the barnyard and rush out to find all four children pointing in mortal terror at some unspeakable threat. "A woim, a woim, a big fuzzy green woim," they would chant in four-part Brooklynese Gregorian. More often than not, the monster wasn't a "woim" at all, but some poor innocent cricket or potato bug.

After a week in Oklahoma, we traveled west to Cisco, Texas, where my mother and sister lived, and where I had spent my teens and early twenties. Cisco was a lazy, sundrenched western town that boasted the world's largest swimming pool and Conrad Hilton's first hotel. During the Ranger oil boom of the twenties, it had reached a population of fifteen thousand, but when the oil played out, it had shrunk to its present size of four thousand.

It was easy to forget Brooklyn, and I found that I could put my old Texas accent on and off like a pair of house slippers. When a waitress would ask, "What'll ya'll have to drink—cawfee or aace tee?" I would automatically reply, "Ah thank ahl have aace tee, pleeze, mayam." The kids would crack up, and Margie would glare. The poor waitress didn't know what was so funny. Soon the children picked up the beat and went around saying things like, "Ah thank ahl taike uh baiuth and go tuh baiud; ahm as tarred as all git out. Must be all that thar sayund." They would tease their cousin Timmie by saying, "Paleeze tawk some more Taxus."

Going back home always took me into the past. My mother's father, the Reverend Franz Steyer, had been a Lutheran minister. Born and educated in Germany, he had written Latin poetry for a pastime, and he had never learned to preach in English. When my mother, Dorothea Steyer, was twenty-eight, she married Christian Frederick Prange, a fifty-eight-year-old widower with seven grown children. There were four children born of this union. I was the first child and the only son.

18

My father was proud of this son born in his old age, and I guess I should be thankful that he didn't name me Isaac, but Erwin was bad enough. Father took me everywhere with him as soon as I was big enough to walk.

"Nice grandson you have there, Mr. Prange."

"That's not my grandson, that's my son," dad would sputter, the gray ends of his handlebar moustache bristling with indignation.

"Oh?" Most of his business acquaintances knew that he had married a young woman after his first wife had died, but they liked to tease him.

When I was two, "Aunt Grace," who was actually my sister-in-law, died suddenly. She lived next-door and had been very close to me. After a short funeral service in the house, Aunt Grace was buried in a rough pine box at the local graveyard. I took it all in, standing in front of the other mourners and holding my mother's hand when they put the lid on the box and lowered it into the hole. When the clods of earth began to fall on the coffin, something happened to me. Up until that point I believed that Aunt Grace would wake up again and get out of the box, and that this was some kind of strange adult game. But when the hole began to fill, I knew I would never again hear her laughter or feel her loving arms around me.

At that moment, a fear of death was born which was to profoundly affect my entire life. That night, before I went to sleep, mother and I talked it out. The dialogue is still preserved in an old baby book in German.

"Mutter, muessen wir alle sterben?" (Mother, must we all die?)

19

"Ja, nur Gott und die Engel nicht." (Yes, all except God and the angels.)

"Brauchen die Engel nicht sterben weil sie Federn haben?" (Don't the angels have to die because they have feathers?)

"Nein, ich glaube nicht." (No, I don't think so.)

"Mutter du wirst der Liebe Gott und ich werde ein Engel dann brauchen wir nicht sterben." (Mother, you be God and I'll be an angel and then we won't have to die.)

The clods dropping on Grace's pine box still echo in my dreams, but they are no longer the voice of doom they once were. We only learn to truly live when we come to terms with death, Spinoza said and Freud after him. But a child cannot cope with the whole cultural and religious burden of Adam's fall.

I developed the habit of compulsive praying to ward off the monsters. It was more of a fear-filled incantation or magic ritual than a real prayer. Sometimes I prayed against the dark unknown for as much as three hours before falling into exhausted sleep. I believed that if I did not pray against every form of enemy every night, I would die before morning. Heaven heard the meaning of the prayers and granted me merciful release from the compulsion.

When I was nine, death scored again. My father died at the age of sixty-eight from a post-operative infection. One shot of penicillin or a few antibiotics might have saved him, but the year was 1926. The family made me kiss his cold cheek in farewell, and again I had to stand front and center at the graveside. After all, it was a son's duty. This time, the sound of the clods was even louder, for in the seven years between gravesides I had learned that there was something worse even than death: hell. Beneath the dirt and the coffin and the earth, an eternal fire waited for sinners—like me.

In the car, returning from Dad's funeral, Mother turned to me and said, "You are now the man of the family." I took her literally, and when Grandfather Steyer gave me a twenty-dollar gold-piece, I went out and bought a sixteen-gauge shotgun that I could barely hold steady and started blasting away at rabbits, ducks, and geese. I also fished and swam in the swift, deep, White River, climbed the giant water tower and did all the things that my father had forbidden me to do. If I was going to die and go to hell, I might as well live it up first. When relatives and neighbors complained, Mother said resignedly, "He's the man of the family now."

In 1928, the Tom Sawyer days were over. We moved to Cisco, in hot, dry, West Texas. I attended parochial school and worked at whatever odd jobs I could find. In the summertime, there were incredibly long, backbreaking days working on some farm for my board and fifty cents a day. Childhood was gone forever. Even with its terrors, there had been some compensations. Anything was better than digging potatoes, shaking peanuts, or baling hay for twelve hours a day.

Two of my mother's brothers were Lutheran clergymen. When Uncle Carl would come to visit us in Cisco, he and I would often sleep outside under the Texas stars. One night he talked to me almost the whole night about the love of Jesus and the joyous reality of God. I had never heard any man talk like that before. Sure, ministers talked about the

THE GIFT IS ALREADY YOURS

love of God in sermons and Bible classes, but it didn't sound real. Uncle Carl seemed to know Jesus in a way that the rest of us didn't—as if He were alive.

And something else: it came through in everything he did and said. You could even hear it when he played the violin. Uncle Carl had a secret. Maybe he himself didn't realize what it was. And it was years after he was dead before I guessed the secret of his abiding joy.

Uncle Ed was a little younger, pastor of the German Lutheran church in Cisco when we first moved there. A mystic in the medieval sense, he became a kind of substitute father figure for me, though he had already had three boys of his own. We shared a great deal as I grew older. About a year before he died in 1958, he began to drop hints about some deep, secret, spiritual experience. He said that he had at last found peace and certainty. His death was a great personal loss to me. I mourned more over him than I had over the death of my own father.

My mother and my Aunt Helen also reflected the deep, mystic spirituality of the Steyer family, and it was passed on to my youngest sister, Christine. But it bypassed me. Everyone was convinced that I would be the lost sheep of the family. I was the one that all of them prayed for. When I developed a taste for alcohol at an early age, the family pulled a few dark skeletons out of the closet to try to frighten me into righteousness, but all the "Jesus talk" only made me uncomfortable.

When I graduated from grade school in 1930, my mother and my pastor approached me with a missionary gleam in their eyes.

22

"Erwin, we have been discussing your future and have decided that you should become a pastor."

By then I knew for certain that I didn't want to be a farmer, but I hadn't really thought about being a pastor.

"Too shy," I protested, not unlike Moses.

"You're still young, and you will grow out of that."

"But I haven't been called." Somewhere I'd heard that expression, and it sounded like a good out.

"Well, how about a parochial schoolteacher?" It sounded harmless enough, and so we finally settled on that.

I was duly enrolled in the brand-new Concordia Lutheran Academy at Austin, Texas, and in September left home for the first time, at the ripe old age of thirteen. The school was beautiful, the classes were small, and the teachers were excellent, all ministers and many with Ph.D.s. But I was homesick, desperately homesick. Despite the many jokes about it, homesickness can be a fearsome ailment, a deep, unhealable wound that many old people even die of, when they are moved into a nursing home.

The years at Austin went swiftly. In my first year, I changed to the ministerial program, because I felt that parochial schoolteachers were second-rate, and I wanted to go first class. I was elected president of the student body in my senior year and was valedictorian of my graduating class. But they weren't really happy years. And after four years, there was still no clear call from God to the ministry, so I began to look for ways to escape. Not finding any, the next year I went to St. John's College in Winfield, Kansas, to continue my studies. There, I became a member of the debating team and won first prize in the college oratory contest. The year was intellectually satisfying, but when we were required to go on a religious canvass, I almost died. How could I talk to anyone about Jesus Christ, when I didn't know Him myself? So far, there had been much talk about Him, but no one had offered to introduce me. I couldn't just walk up and say, "Jesus, I'm Erve Prange, and I'd like to know You better, especially since I'm going to be one of Your ministers."

The following year, the elders in my home congregation let me off the hook. They refused to endorse my request for financial aid, saying that we already had too many ministers and that my mother and sisters needed my help.

It was 1933, the depths of the great depression. I was able to find a seasonal job working on the local golf course. In between, I worked in a feedmill, in the harvests, and on pipelines, clearing right-of-way. After one year, the elders relented, and I got ready to go back to Winfield. At the last moment, I changed my mind. I would stay at the golf course—until Pearl Harbor. It was a mistake that I lived to regret.

The time of remembering had passed. July was almost gone, and we had to get back to Brooklyn. Before we left, Mother asked, "What can we here do for you there? We worry about you. It's so far away, and the things you tell about the city are so frightening. It's all so different from the way you grew up—and Margie, too."

"Well, you can pray for us," I said, almost automatically.

"How long?" Mother was always something of a literalist.

"How about like Martin Luther, four hours a day?" I

replied, somewhat facetiously, I'm afraid, and never dreaming she'd take me seriously. Mother and some of her female friends had started a Bible-study group the year before at my suggestion.

"What shall we pray for?"

"The Holy Spirit," I answered, again without thinking. I didn't even know who the Holy Spirit was, but those words were to prove to be the most fateful of my life.

We went back by way of Houston, New Orleans, and Florida. Even though I had practiced setting up the tent in Kansas, I kept finding excuses not to camp, until I ran out of rationalizations in Panama City, Florida. It was very late. And very hot. We chose a site on the shores of beautiful Dead Fish Bay. While I fumbled and bumbled with the equipment, the children waded in Dead Fish Bay. The bay was correctly named; the aroma did not leave them for two weeks.

I could not get the tent up right. Then the stove wouldn't stay lit, and then the mosquitoes struck. They seemed to be as big—and as busy—as hummingbirds. The children began to howl, and we stuffed them into the station wagon. By this time Margie and I weren't speaking to each other.

After we had done all we could, we gave up, embraced, and began to laugh, even though Stephen was still crying. I took pictures of this historic occasion—the first (and last) time that we camped as a family. Years later, in Montana, the boys used the tent to camp out in our front yard, so the money wasn't all wasted.

Back in Brooklyn, the mosquito bites and the fragrance of Dead Fish Bay gradually subsided and the summer of '63 became a memory. But back in Cisco, the little prayer group kept on praying, and the wheels of heaven began to turn. That is the great risk of prayer: not that God might say no, but that He might say yes, for we do not know what we pray.

III

HEAD OR HEART?

In Romans 7:21–24, St. Paul describes his personal civil war. The battle between Spirit and flesh was for him not just a cosmic struggle but something that took place inside of him each day. His own body was the battlefield from which he longed to escape.

My private war in 1963 was between my head and heart. My Prussian ancestors had bred into me a deep distrust of the emotions. Man had to live by reason; living at the "gut" level was undisciplined and self-indulgent. To a degree, these ancestors were right; when men live just on the level of feelings, a moral breakdown results.

On the other hand, we cannot live by reason alone. We cannot truly relate to God and each other on the intellectual level. For me, words were not merely means of communicating, but sharp weapons to win the upper hand. I used words, not to relate, but to hold people at arm's length. Once in a while, a wise friend would say, "Come out from behind those big words, Erve, and tell me what you feel."

God was a verbal symbol. He was the supreme intellect, the ultimate philosopher. I could read and discuss Him in half-a-dozen languages, but I was like a child in the nursery spelling God with the wrong blocks. Most of what I said about Him meant nothing to me, because I didn't know Him.

My approach to the problems of the church in the inner city was intellectual. I read books, made surveys, and developed programs. We called meetings and talked and talked and talked. I also began to write articles about the problem of the inner-city church. They proved to be highly popular, fed my overstuffed ego, made people feel guilty, and changed nothing.

We also acted. We tried Lutheran "Peace Corps" task forces, coffeehouses and community action programs. We tamed and adopted one of the toughest Brooklyn street gangs and renamed them "The St. Mark's Celestians." We started AA chapters and tried to do something about the drug problem. We started a Spanish language service and reopened the parochial school. We tried every gimmick the church had come up with, including the Cottage Bible Plan.

All of these things helped, but something vital was missing: people's lives were not being transformed. Where was the power of God? To be sure, the church had a societal responsibility which had been neglected, but its real mission was to radically change lives. Where did the Spirit of God fit into all of this? Did He merely endorse our programs, or was He indeed the creative initiative of God?

In September, I heard about something called the Baptism in the Holy Spirit for the first time. My informant told me that the Spirit came through the laying on of hands and not through the intellect. There were wild rumors about speaking in tongues and about miracles and about Lutherans praising God.

I was skeptical, and yet my heart was strangely warmed. What if it were true? What if a man could actually experience the presence of God like some of the New Testament writers had done? I felt a deep hunger and longing for the reality of God. The pages of the Bible had to come alive. I wanted the Word to become flesh in my own life space. But if it hadn't happened to me before, how could it happen now at this late date?

In November, a meeting was convened at Trinity Lutheran Church in Manhattan, the subject of which was the Pentecostal movement that was beginning to appear in the denominational churches. This meeting brought together the kind of human potpourri that only New York's Lower East Side could produce. There were Quakers and Catholics, Baptists and Zen Buddhists, Agnostics, Pentecostals, Presbyterians and Lutherans, plus assorted artists, mystics, and hippies looking for a new kind of trip.

The meeting was conducted by a fresh-faced young Presbyterian minister, and as he spoke, I began to sharpen my theological and intellectual talons. A young Pentecostal from Teen Challenge began to describe the miracles happening among drug addicts in my own neighborhood. This interested me immensely, but his thick Oklahoma accent, his dogmatic assertions, and his anti-Catholic bias turned me off. I decided that if he had the Baptism in the Holy Spirit, I didn't want it.

Then a beautiful young Roman Catholic actress spoke. Her eyes shone, and her face lit up whenever she mentioned the name of Jesus. She looked exactly like a girl in love for the first time. When she spoke about Jesus, the very sound of her voice made Him real. And suddenly, for the first time in my life, I actually felt the presence of God.

Others, including several Lutherans, gave their testimony. They all had the same shining eyes and the same excitement in their voices. They just couldn't seem to stop talking about the Lord. My eyes were getting a little misty, and there was a faint tingling in my body. This had to stop; I was getting emotional. The heart was taking over the head.

The enemy was disturbed. He pumped up all my intellectual pride. I would trot out my erudition and impress those present. If there was any resistance, I would simply overwhelm it with my superior theology. After all, this was just the same old emotional Fundamentalist claptrap. I simply had never been this close to it before.

"Pentecostals are fanatics, and God is a God of order and dignity," I kept saying. My profound logic and devastating oratory soon emptied the room. The magic moment was gone, and so was the audience. Erve Prange's rhetoric had even driven away the Holy Spirit, yet strangely, there was no satisfaction in the victory. On the contrary, I felt utterly miserable, like I had just taken a flower in my hand and crushed it.

I couldn't get those sparkling eyes and shining faces out of my mind. I had to face it: these people had something I didn't have. Something I wanted desperately. But a highly trained, self-esteeming intellect does not give up easily. If I had to have this thing, it was going to be on my intellect's terms. I took out my set of Kittel's *Theological Dictionary of the New Testament* and read hundreds of pages in German on the gifts of the Spirit. I read everything I could lay my hands on about the Holy Spirit and tongues, and there wasn't much. Lutheran theologians had no doctrine of the Holy Spirit worthy of the name. The Roman Catholics were pretty much in the same boat. The Holy Spirit was the missing person of the Trinity.

Why? Maybe because a father was a father and Jesus was a man, but what do you do with a dove or a ghost? But the Holy Spirit was supposed to be God in the present tense. He was the executive secretary of the Godhead. How could He possibly be overlooked? Then where was the actual point of contact, Means of Grace—water baptism, faith, the laying on of hands, or God forbid, tongues?

And what about this "tongues" business anyhow? In the seminary, when we came to I Corinthians 14, the professor made us all chant together, "Bobelty, bobelty, bobelty." That little exercise in nonsense syllables was supposed to settle the "tongues" question once and for all. "Let all things be done decently and in order." That was the core of all Lutheran theology and practice. No one seemed to be bothered by the words immediately preceding: "Do not forbid speaking in tongues."

Some people collect stamps; I collected languages. I had a tin ear for music, as my congregation could readily attest, but the Lord had given me a good ear for languages. Such was my fluency that even though both my parents were born in the United States, I was sent on underground missions in Europe during World War II. Were these strange sounds called "tongues" really a language? Did they come from man or from God, and what had they to do with the Holy Spirit? I had never heard anyone speak in tongues,

31

but my intellectual and linguistic curiosity could hardly be more aroused. I was determined to get to the bottom of this thing.

The opportunity was to come sooner than I expected. Late in November, I learned that a Lutheran charismatic group met regularly in the home of Ron Haines on Long Island, and I received an invitation to attend a Friday night meeting.

Two members of Trinity Lutheran Church drove with me to the Long Island meeting. When we arrived, some forty people had already gathered. Most of them were Lutheran lay people. But there was something completely different about these Lutherans. First, they were friendly; second they were joyful; but most amazing of all, they were talking about the Lord! They weren't in church, and it wasn't even Sunday. All of them were carrying Bibles, too. Lutheran Bible classes were dying, and it took the average Lutheran 112 years to lead someone to Christ, but these people were voluntarily witnessing and studying the Bible, and apparently newcomers were meeting the Lord almost every week.

Something had to be wrong. Sure enough, I didn't see any Lutheran pastors around. When the singing started, I *knew* that something was wrong. The average Lutheran service sounds like a particularly tragic funeral. The hymns in our hymnal are excellent, but usually they are sung very slowly, without enthusiasm or conviction. Sometimes, almost no one would sing, especially if the hymn was unfamiliar. At times, my congregation would simply glare at me as if to say, "All right, Pastor. You picked it, let's hear you sing it."

This group was really different. When they sang Martin Luther's "A Mighty Fortress Is Our God," I thought the

Reformation had started all over again. They made the old Bach chorales sound like Baptist camp-meeting hymns, and when they came to "Praise to the Lord, the Almighty, the King of Creation," I began to believe they actually meant it.

I shook my head. They couldn't be Lutherans—they just couldn't. People were smiling, and there was real joy on their faces, as well as in their singing. It was a Lutheran tradition that to come into the presence of God you had to put on your best clothes and your saddest face. Lutherans were permitted to holler as loud as anyone else at a football game, but to show joy in worship was near blasphemy. Somehow Lutherans had never managed to get beyond Good Friday. Psychiatrists said they could always spot a Lutheran by the guilty look on his face.

I sat in the front row, clerical collar and all, and suddenly one of the leaders addressed me.

"Pastor Prange, how are you this evening? I haven't seen you since the meeting in Manhattan."

I swallowed. I didn't want to be reminded about that meeting which I had more or less ruined.

"I'm fine, just fine," I said, trying to show it by smiling. "I'm here investigating this new movement."

"Would you like to receive the Baptism in the Holy Spirit?"

"Yes, I guess so."

"Would you like to come forward for ministry?"

"No." *In front of all these lay people? He had to be kidding!* "But I would like to hear someone speak in tongues. I've never heard it, and I am interested in languages."

Suddenly there was low hum in the room, and as I found

out later, they were singing in the Spirit. It wasn't unpleasant. I thought I picked up certain familiar words. I began to focus on the woman sitting near me. She was definitely singing in Latin. I heard quite a few of the words; it sounded like one of the Psalms.

I was a little shaken up. Was it really Latin? Maybe she was an ex-nun or something. She might have been a high school Latin teacher. Yes, that had to be it. But why was I so agitated? Was this stuff beginning to get to me?

I was tempted to give the leader a hard time, but it was getting late, and I had a long drive ahead of me. On the way back to Manhattan, we said very little. After I dropped off the two members of Trinity Lutheran who had accompanied me, I drove across the Williamsburg bridge to Brooklyn, arriving home about midnight.

The whole house was quiet. Even Jefferson Street was quiet for a change. But as tired as I was, I couldn't sleep. I thought about going into the church and praying about the whole thing, but decided instead on a couple of double bourbons.

No doubt about it, there was a tremendous conflict brewing inside of me. I wanted to believe all of this, and yet I didn't. It was just too good to be true. God didn't work like that. The Spirit didn't come through the laying on of hands, and Long Island housewives didn't sing in Latin. These Lutherans were just catching up on their long-suppressed emotional life, that was all.

When sleep finally came, I was troubled by many dreams. I saw the clods falling on Aunt Grace's grave again, and this time the old teenage dream about hell came in technicolor. Everything seemed to be a huge kaleidoscope of rapidly moving, brilliantly colored confusion. I changed from a giant to a tiny midget and seemed to be plunging headlong into an eternal abyss. Solar systems and galaxies went shooting by, and then there was deep darkness. And infinite emptiness.

All of a sudden, it seemed that the emptiness was inside of me. Door after door of my innermost self was opened, revealing only debris and dust. When the last door was opened, my personal holy of holies proved to be as empty and dark as the rest. All around were dreadful secrets and horrible memories, but no light or life. Where was God? Wasn't He supposed to be inside of me? Where was the Spirit if my body was His temple?

IV

DECEMBER 7

"On this day, twenty-two years ago, the air arm of the Japanese fleet attacked Pearl Harbor." The clock radio was warming to the seven o'clock news.

Groggy and a little hung over, I turned the radio down in order not to wake Margie. On Sunday, December 7, 1941, I had been sitting in my golf shop in Texas. We had been to church, and after a big dinner, I was waiting for the first Sunday afternoon golfers to show up. Life was secure, and I enjoyed my job as manager of the country club and golf course.

When the radio in the pro shop first announced the attack on Pearl Harbor, I thought it was some kind of hoax. I was an aviation cadet in the Army Air Corps reserves and had been taking flying lessons under the Civilian Pilot Training program—a neat arrangement, since the airport was right next to the golf course. Any day now, I was going to land right on the golf course. I had the spot all picked out. Boy, would that shake up the members! Suddenly, it was me who was shook up.

On December 7, 1963, I got up, took a quick shower, and

started to shave. The twenty-two years since Pearl Harbor had taken their toll. Besides losing a lot of hair, I had put on about twenty-five pounds. I remembered a snapshot taken when I was in pre-flight training at Maxwell Field, Alabama. I actually had looked handsome then, staring up into the wild blue yonder with unclouded blue eyes. This morning, my eyes were bloodshot, and I wore bifocals.

While I was fixing my breakfast, I remembered still another December 7. On December 7, 1942, I was scheduled to solo. For some reason, I was nervous and shot two bad landings, and so the great event had to be postponed until the next day. My instructor was young. He had already washed out two of his three students. I was the only one left. Sometimes I felt sorry for both of us. We worked so hard, risking our necks, just so I could learn to be an airborne killer. I could have been a chaplain by then, if I had gone on to seminary. What was I doing training to be a bomber pilot?

I did solo the next day, without incident, and began to accumulate solo hours. Air sickness kept plaguing me. Time after time I had to clean up the plane and then report to the psychiatrist. He always wanted to know how I felt about my childhood and my parents. I never did tell him the problem—or my dream. By now I had developed an absolute terror of death, and the fact that students were being killed every week didn't help.

One day my instructor told me to go up to 3,500 feet and do a two-and-a-half-turn spin to the left and then go back to 3,000 and do a two-turn spin to the right. He intended to watch from the safety of the ground. By then, these spins were routine. What wasn't routine, was that, unbeknown to us, a very fat female ground-crew member had leaned on my right-wing trim tab when she gassed up the plane.

I went up to 3,500 and did my two-and-a-half-turn spin to the left. No problem, except that the plane seemed to react somewhat sluggishly. Something told me to cheat a little and go back to 3,500 instead of just 3,000 for the two-turn spin to the right.

At the end of the second spin, I went through the normal recovery procedure. But nothing happened. Alarmed, I did it again. Still no response. I began to panic as the plane went into a flat spin and came down like a falling leaf. Nothing helped, and in desperation, I unbuckled my seat belt and crawled out of the open cockpit and over the side, preparing to jump. By this time, I was less than five hundred feet from the ground. My chute could never open in time. It was too late to jump, too late to pray, too late even to repent. And so I dangled there, hanging by my hands to the rim of the cockpit, as the plane went round and round, down and down. I remembered, then, the voice of doom that had come once in the dream: "He who puts his hand to the plow and turns back is not worthy of me." So this was my punishment for leaving my ministerial studies! But God had never called me! I looked down and sobbed; the ground was only two hundred feet below, and I would soon be hitting the tops of the tallest trees.

Suddenly, the plane righted itself and went into a gentle glide. It couldn't be! It was. With strength I didn't know I had left, I hoisted myself back up on the wing and climbed back into the cockpit, grasping the controls and opening the throttle all the way. I yanked back on the stick—just in time to clear a huge Arkansas oak. Three times I circled the field before my knees would stop knocking. When I finally landed, I got out, took a huge handful of earth, and ate it. The trees, the bushes, and even the weeds were transformed. The air was like champagne, and the wind sang hallelujah. I was alive!

God seemed to be speaking to me that day. He had saved my life for something, and He wanted me out of the pilot program. I was more than ready to buy that, but the Air Corps wasn't. They told me to forget it and keep on flying. The incident obviously wasn't my fault; it could have happened to anyone. In fact, they were proud of how well I had handled myself! Little did they know how scared I had been.

Cleaning up my breakfast dishes, twenty-one years later, I thought about one other incident in my mercurial flying career. That time it *had* been my fault. We were flying in Arkansas, and one day I decided to buzz Crocketts Bluff, the place where I was born. Flat-hatting was strictly forbidden, but it was a beautiful clear day, and I couldn't get lost.

I had a ball! Carving graceful Immelmanns and chandelles in the azure sky, I buzzed the house, the barn, the store, and everything that moved. I screamed in low along the river, scaring the shelldiggers in their motorboats and almost taking the roofs off the houseboats.

On the way back, the impossible happened. I got lost. I finally located the airport at Memphis, Tennessee, but instead of landing to gas up, and getting put on report, I decided to try to make it back to the base at Helena. My fuel began to get very low, and as it did, I began to realize what a fool I had been. Realizing it, however, did not reverse the downward direction of my fuel gauges. One wing tank went dry, and I switched to the other. There was less than a quarter of a tank left, and I still couldn't see Helena. I thought of parachuting, but underneath I could see nothing but impenetrable Mississippi River Swamp.

Finally I decided to ride the plane down and take my chances on a crash landing in the brush. Just as the last gas was used up and the engine coughed and was silent, I saw a huge green field ahead and slightly to the left. Some smoke from a brush fire gave me the wind direction I needed. I coasted, confident of a perfect landing—until when I was about twenty feet above the ground, I saw water shining up through the grass.

There was nothing left to do but stall the plane out at that altitude. I jerked the nose up, and the plane plunked down in the swamp. The wheels hit and stuck. The plane rocked back and forth on its axis, but didn't move one foot forward. Every time it rocked, my head banged the instrument panel.

I must have been unconscious for about thirty minutes. When I came to, a black teenager was peeking over the side of the cockpit.

"Hey, white boy," he said, "this here ain't no landin' field."

"You are so right," I said. "Now where is the nearest telephone, so I can pass on that bit of information?"

I trudged one mile through the mud in my heavy flying clothes and found a telephone. The base immediately sent out a rescue plane with gasoline and a test pilot. They landed in a dry corner of the field. The lieutenant walked up to me, and I saluted as if we were on the parade ground. He inspected the plane.

"Mister! Where are your tracks?"

"Sir?"

"Where are your tracks?"

"Tracks, sir?"

"Yes, tracks, man! How did you get this plane in this field?"

"Flew it in, sir; it was too heavy to carry."

"Don't you get flippant with me. There are no wheel tracks. You could not have flown that plane into this mud without leaving tracks."

"Sir, I guess I sort of dropped it in."

He shook his head. "Absolutely impossible. It can't be done."

"I'm sorry, sir."

"You should be! You have done something which I cannot and will not believe."

After a great deal of hauling and winching, they managed to fly the plane out of a dry section of the field. I took a check ride and passed, but I had decided that this was it. This time the Lord had spoken plainly. I washed myself out and ended my flying career. It was obvious that God had other plans for me. After the war, I learned that more than half my class had become casualties.

After I left the Air Corps, I was sent to the University of St. Louis for a crash course in advanced German. In five months, I was classified as an interpreter-investigator and sent to England. Shortly after the Normandy invasion, we landed in France and marched through the rubble of Saint-Lô toward Germany. The Battle of the Bulge stopped us for a while, but early in '45, we were with Patton, rolling for Germany.

I was with an advance military government team, and our job was to organize municipal governments in Germany in the wake of Patton's tanks. Things were moving so fast that my commanding officer and I went ahead alone and left the rest of the team behind. In one day, we set up nineteen new civic governments. We had to quickly provide for public health, public safety, and communications, as well as pick up all weapons and ammunition still in the hands of Germans.

At about three one afternoon, we were in a German town of about thirty thousand that had been taken less than two hours before. The captain and I issued proclamations at city hall, appointed a new mayor and police chief, and gave orders for all weapons and ammunition to be brought into the city hall courtyard. As it began to come in by the truckload, we realized that the town had been a German ammunition dump.

In the meantime, the captain had sent a lieutenant out to find a billet for us. The lieutenant, a lawyer who spoke just enough German to confuse friend and foe alike, was too proud to use an interpreter, so I had stayed with the captain. The pile of weapons and ammunition continued to grow. Some of the truck drivers seemed to be very careless about backing up onto live bombs and mines, and we began to get more than a bit nervous. Just at that moment, the lieutenant returned.

"Captain," he reported, "I'm afraid I just can't seem to find a billet in this town."

The captain, a New England salt, blew up. "Lieutenant!" he shouted, "we are winning a war. We have just captured this town. We are the victors and you are telling me there is no place in this whole town for us to stay? That's what I get for having a dumb shyster on my team. With your lousy German, they probably thought you were a Russian—or maybe even a Japanese.

"Come on, Prange! We'll have a billet in less than a minute. Thank God I've got at least one man on the team who speaks decent German!" With that, he grabbed me by the arm and hauled me down the street, on the double.

We had run a couple of blocks when suddenly behind us the whole world seemed to blow up, and we were knocked flat. When we went back to inspect the disaster, we found that all the ammunition in the city square had exploded at once. The city hall, where we had been just moments before, was a shambles. The hospital across the street had all the windows and doors blown out, and most of the patients had been blown out of their beds. The remains of some forty men were gathered and placed into one bushel basket.

I turned away and began to weep. Blood was running in the gutter. The shrieks that filled the air sounded like the cries of damned souls. Death, the skullfaced archenemy, was grinning at me from every side.

How could one deal with him? You couldn't face him, and you couldn't run away. During the Battle of the Bulge, I had even volunteered (but had not been accepted) to be parachuted behind the lines. I was so frightened that I had determined to take death by the throat and conquer him in hand-to-hand combat. And now this. Had we left three seconds later, had we not left on the dead run, had that lieutenant not been so proud of his German . . .

V

THE GIFT IS ALREADY YOURS

Nine o'clock—time to get ready for the confirmation class. Somehow this was one of the most difficult parts of my whole ministry. Every year we were confirming thirty or so young people—right out of the church. It had gotten to be a kind of graduation exercise, because after every confirmation, half of the class would gradually drift away from the church.

I had no solution, and neither did anyone else. The church tried early confirmation, it tried late confirmation, and sometimes none at all. Despite every gimmick and program, the rate of loss remained the same.

In the early Church, confirmation had been set up in order that those baptized with water as infants might receive the Holy Spirit in a formal way. In early German Lutheranism, confirmation had been the public sign that religious instruction was at an end and the teenager might work full time in the field or in the house. In American Lutheranism, confirmation was supposed to be a public adult assent to infant baptism.

Confirmation would have been the ideal time to ask for a

public and personal commitment to Christ, particularly as conversion is a normal adolescent phenomenon. Lutherans, however, tended to be wary of "decision theology," and it is possible to be an elder or a pastor in the Lutheran church without ever having made a real commitment to Christ.

Jonathan Edwards said in his book on the revival in New England that the "cold dead saints" sent more souls to hell than natural men. He also said that unconverted church members were far more stubborn in opposing the movings of the Spirit than unbelievers. His words were to prove prophetically true when spiritual renewal began to move into the church centuries later.

I still had an hour before my class was scheduled to arrive. In defeat, and utterly devoid of inspiration, I felt I might as well go into the church and pray—it couldn't hurt. As I got up from my desk, I realized I was angry. And frustrated and bitter. I was "a man of God," but it had been so long since I had felt His presence that my attitude was almost that He didn't exist. It had gotten to the point that I couldn't do anything for Him, and He seemed powerless to help me. Somehow I sensed that I was going to have it out with God on this December 7.

The door of my study led directly into the church. As I went in, the peace and majesty of that place made me feel small and somehow privileged to even be there. The ceiling was fifty-five feet high, and the back of the balcony, which raised the seating capacity to more than 1,300 worshipers, was filled by a giant five-rank pipe organ. It was said that the organ was capable of shattering the huge stained-glass windows that reached almost from floor to ceiling. Up in the

45

tower were twenty tons of carillon bells and a huge Seth Thomas clock with four faces, and hands eight feet long. The narthex was a museum containing beautiful mementos of a glorious Germanic past. And presiding in magnificent bronze splendor was August Emil Frey, the fiery little Swiss pastor (1868–1904) who, if attendance was off, would stop the service and go out into the local beer halls to round up his flock. In addition, the church council and building committee of 1891 had immortalized themselves in letters of gold on two huge tablets of stone. The beautiful but worn mosaic floor spelled out in German, "Dedicated by the Children."

The pulpit was elaborately carved out of highly polished red cherry. It was placed above and in back of the altar as a symbol of the high status which Lutherans give to preaching. Entry to the pulpit was gained from a hidden panel on the side of the altar. In spite of careful directions, many a confused guest preacher had to be fetched as he mistakenly wandered into the parsonage or out into the school yard. One guest even made it out onto Jefferson Street before I could catch him.

As my eyes swept over the beautiful nave with all its rich symbolism, I shook my head. How did I get here? How did I fit into all of this?

When the war was over, I had been in no big hurry to get home, so I signed on for a tour of duty as a War Department Civilian with the Restitution Branch of Military Government. The work was challenging, and the pay very good.

In the beginning of 1949, I returned to the United States

with a fistful of war bonds. I didn't have the faintest idea what I was going to do, but I did plan to go to school on the G.I. Education Bill.

The ministry was the farthest thing from my mind, though all through the war years I had had the same dream almost every night—a dream in which I finished college and seminary and entered the ministry.

The war had left me with a fair-sized beer-thirst, but with no other visible scars. The world was my oyster. I could become just about anything I wanted to, including a doctor. Maybe I would be a lawyer or get a doctorate in languages. I was interested in journalism and history, too.

Then suddenly, after a seventeen-year delay, the call came to the ministry! How do you know when God calls you? Usually, you just know. No visions or voices or fiery letters in the sky. No angel messenger comes to inform you that you have been invited to be one of God's ministers. You just know.

If the call is genuine, something else happens: God begins to rearrange the furniture of your life to make the call possible. In my case, it took some extensive rearranging. First, I wrote to our late-vocation seminary in Springfield, Illinois. I was promptly accepted. That was too easy.

Mother and I were still living on the golf course. I had agreed to run the country club for one more year before leaving for school. Bill Backus, a senior in Concordia Seminary in St. Louis, stopped by during the Christmas holidays. He had boarded with my mother during his internship in Cisco.

I proudly showed him my acceptance to Springfield.

47

"You don't mean to tell me you're going to Springfield?" Somehow he made it sound like an institution for the mentally retarded.

"Why, what's wrong with Springfield?" I was hurt, having expected him to be enthusiastic about my call to the ministry.

"There's only one decent seminary in the Lutheran Church, and that's Concordia, St. Louis. Now tear up that stupid acceptance and send for an application to St. Louis." Bill always was a persuasive guy. At 4:00 A.M., after we had shared a couple of six-packs, I did what he said.

Strangely enough, I began to get very enthusiastic letters from Concordia—all signed by the Dean. It sounded as if he could hardly wait until I got there. So in September of 1950, I loaded up my brand-new Studebaker and headed for St. Louis.

There was no brass band to meet me, but the seminary was unbelievably beautiful. I kept pinching myself, half-expecting to wake up and find that it was only the same old dream I'd had all those years.

The Dean had to pinch himself, too. After I had been there about a week, he called me into his office and said bluntly, "Would you mind telling me just how you got into this seminary?"

"But Dean, you wrote me all those nice letters this summer—"

"I've been in Europe all summer. I've never even heard of you."

"Well, who's been writing those letters and signing your name?" I protested, my heart seeping down through the stone floor.

"Now I'm beginning to get the picture. My secretary—Let's see, Mr. Prange, how old are you? Never mind. Since you're here, you might as well stay for a while. You did very well on the tests, as it happens. But you are on probation, and you've got to make up every one of the credits you are lacking."

As far as I know, I'm still on probation. To this day, whenever I see that Dean I try to blend into the shrubbery.

The seminary years were swift and pleasant, but they were far more intellectual than spiritual. There was one small liturgical group that conducted private devotions in the prayer chapel. In fact, some of them celebrated all the canonical hours just like medieval monks. A few of my friends belonged to this group and often urged me to join them. I did several times, but I couldn't see what thrill they got out of reciting those ancient liturgical forms. The singing in the chapel was good, and once in a while, there would be an inspiring sermon. Most of the time, however, chapel was sheer duty. I felt very guilty for not wanting to go and not enjoying it more.

Everyone else seemed to be about on the same level. They said the right things and did the right things, but it all seemed to be taking place at the head level and not the gut level.

I was happy, I was at peace, and I was looking forward to entering the ministry. Was there supposed to be more than this? The verse on the wall of the prayer chapel haunted me: "I have been crucified with Christ: it is no longer I who live, but Christ who lives in me; and the life I now live in the flesh I live by faith in the Son of God" (Gal. 2:20 RSV).

What did that *really* mean? Was there anyone on campus

49

in whom Christ really seemed to live? There was one professor who seemed very Christlike—until he lost his temper. A few of the students did talk about Christ quite a bit, calling Him Jesus, as if they knew Him well enough to call Him by His first name, but they were labeled fanatics. Once in a while, a student would come back from his summer vicarage acting like he had been converted, but that would soon wear off.

"By faith"—maybe that was the answer. We were supposed to live by faith and not by experience. But if Christ really lived in us, as that passage so boldly stated, then shouldn't there be some kind of experience of that life? After all, life was experience and not just concept or faith.

In my third year, I met a slender Oklahoma brunette who was a senior at Valparaiso University. After a whirlwind courtship, commuting the 500 miles between St. Louis and Chicago like we were going downtown shopping, we were married on March 28, 1953. That summer I took over a vacancy at Elim Lutheran church in St. Louis County, and we moved into the parsonage.

That fourth year at the seminary was busy. All at once I had a wife, a church, and a B.D. thesis to write. In the spring, Elim gave me a direct call, and on June 20, 1954, I was ordained and installed as their regular pastor.

During the following year, our first daughter, Karen, was born, and the congregation built a new church with their own hands. A year later, Diane was born, and we rebuilt the parsonage. I enrolled in graduate school at the seminary, part time. My career was moving along all the right channels.

Then came the call from St. Mark's in Brooklyn, New

York. Who needed New York? I sent the call back. A second call arrived. Shortly thereafter, my telephone rang. It was New York. The call committee from St. Mark's was on the line. We talked ninety dollars' worth. They finally persuaded me to accept a plane ticket and come and look them over. They had heard of me through a former roommate at the seminary who had taken a parish in Manhattan. My old roommate wanted me nearby. St. Mark's wanted a minister who was fluent in German. What did God want? Did that *really* matter?

It was my first commercial plane flight. Snow delayed the takeoff from Lambert Field in St. Louis for two hours. When we finally landed at Idlewild in New York, I was overwhelmed by everything. Those who have never been to New York—or have never lived anywhere else—simply cannot imagine how different it is. To me, New York had a frightening reputation and managed to live up to every bit of it. Taxi drivers, waiters, porters, telephone operators, and police all seemed united in a conspiracy to thoroughly intimidate all visitors—especially me.

That night, I met with the council and voters of St. Mark's. Part of the meeting was conducted in German. They wanted to be sure of one thing, that my German was as fluent as they had heard it was. Whether I was a good preacher or even believed in God was relatively unimportant, once that fact had been established.

When the council conducted me on a tour through the church, I had to admit I was impressed. And then, as I looked at the organ, the bells, and the windows, a deep peace settled over me. I knew this was where God wanted me.

But now, on December 7, 1963, standing in that same nave, I wasn't so sure. As I knelt to the right of the marble angel, I heard myself saying, "God, You and I are going to have it out right now. Either You are going to become real, or I am going to give up this farce. You can have it all back, bells, organ, stained-glass windows—and Brooklyn, too."

At that moment, I imagined that hell for ministers must be listening forever to tapes of their own sermons. There were five steps down from the top of the pulpit to the floor level, but there might have been five million. What an infinite distance there was between those grandiose proclamations of God's power and the petty frustrations of everyday life! How could a man think he was passing out the bread of life every Sunday and still remain so utterly hungry himself? I was empty, and I knew it. This was the end of the line.

All at once, a voice seemed to come from nowhere and everywhere. It was clear and deep and distinct, neither thunder nor whisper.

"The gift is already yours. Reach out and take it."

I couldn't breathe, let alone move. Had I just heard what I thought I— I knew I had. But what gift, where? Obediently, my eyes shut tight. I stretched out my hands toward the altar, palms up. At the same time, I opened my mouth, because my jaws were beginning to tighten.

In an instant, there was a sudden shift of dimensions, and God became real. A spirit of pure love pervaded the church and drenched me like rain. God wasn't just "out there"; He was near, as near as my own spirit. He was beating in my heart, flowing through my blood, breathing in my lungs, and thinking in my brain. Every cell in my body, every nerve end, tingled with the fire of His presence. The whole church, even the worn rugs and peeling walls, looked brand-new.

I, too, was fresh and new. I felt forgiven and cleansed. A lifetime load of guilt had evaporated like fog in the morning sun. Then I noticed that I was praying in a new language of praise.

It had all been so simple and easy. Why hadn't it happened before? For the first time in my life, God was an actual experience and not merely a symbol or a concept. I felt like shouting, "God, where have You been all these years? Why did You suddenly come out of the shadows this morning? What did I do differently today?"

I wanted to rush out into the street and tell the world, "Stop the traffic, stop the trains, stop what you're doing and listen: God is *real!* He's more real than things or people. He is life. He is love. He is joy! I know, because He's inside me and all around me. He is everywhere, and He wants to become real for everyone!"

I wanted to spread the great news, but just then the giant clock in the tower bonged ten times and brought me back from the eternal to the present. A confirmation class was waiting.

VI

THE HONEYMOON OF THE SPIRIT

After most turning-point spiritual experiences, God allows us to have a honeymoon where nearly everything is perfect. The spiritual honeymoon is characterized by peace, joy, and the instant resolution of previous problems. It is the perfect time to make a complete break with the past and start a brand-new life in God.

Unfortunately, the honeymoon does not last forever. It's as long or as short as it needs to be. We are here to grow and to serve, and not merely to celebrate.

The days after December 7 were crammed with preparations for Christmas. This was a joyous season for merchants and children, but a time of extra work for ministers. Not only had Christmas been commercialized by the world, but it had also been over-sentimentalized by the church. The baby Jesus isn't nearly as demanding as the glorified Christ.

Those who made the symbolic journey to the empty manger and the empty tomb every year disturbed me. Germans were especially guilty of this. We had many Christmas-Easter pilgrims on our membership roster, and sometimes I would strike out at them in my holiday sermons.

Margie asked, "Why do you spoil the celebration for everyone else by just preaching against the part-time pilgrims?"

"But look at them," I said, "with their pious postures, tears streaming down their cheeks, and liquor on their breath. It's blasphemy, that's what it is!"

"Erve, stop trying to be God."

Wow! Before, that would really have made me angry. I would have told her off, but good. Now I just smiled.

"Well, I guess you're right. If God can't change them, how can I?"

This Christmas, everything was different. The old German and English carols, the corny programs, and all the chintzy decorations—they were beautiful. Nothing could spoil this Christmas for me, because Christ had just been born in my heart. As I walked the streets of Manhattan, not even Macy's loudspeakers blaring out "White Christmas" could drown out the new song in my soul. My new Christmas carol went something like this, "I'm alive, God is real, He loves me, and all is right with the world."

The wind seemed to join in, and even the taxis and the trains were praising God. Garbage cans were clanging amen, while auto horns blared loud hallelujahs. The touch of angel wings hovered around the mighty skyscrapers, and every raindrop sparkled like Bethlehem's star.

During Christmas week, Margie and I were guests of Pastor and Mrs. George Kraus for a special performance of Handel's *Messiah* at Carnegie Hall. George had a neighboring parish in Brooklyn, and he and Helen were our best friends. They provided what little social life we had outside the parish. George was very gregarious, and although he had some reservations about the charismatic renewal, he was in favor of anything that made people happy, including the Holy Spirit. Helen was very much interested in my experience, since, like most pastor's wives, she usually saw only the worst side of the ministry.

While I had been stationed in Stuttgart, Germany, I had attended the Stuttgart opera about twice a month. I thought the Stuttgart orchestra was about the finest in the world, but it could not compare with the orchestra that played in Carnegie Hall. The *Messiah* was my favorite oratorio, and the performance of Christmas week 1963 had to be the best in the history of music.

It was a foretaste of heaven. Several times I almost wanted to shout out loud, "Stop the music! I can't stand any more! Flesh and blood cannot inherit eternal life." My emotional and spiritual switchboards were about to burn out; I simply couldn't process any more joy.

This was pure musical praise, especially the great "Hallelujah Chorus." I could have listened to it forever. That night in Carnegie Hall, a tiny fraction of what "eye hath not seen nor ear heard," broke through the clouds of heaven. I began to understand why the Book of Revelation pictures paradise in terms of song and praise. In the full reality of the presence of God, man can only respond in the highest form of expression that God has given him. The angels sang the announcement of Christ's birth. No other medium except the heavenly choir could have carried the glory of that message to earth.

The December Long Island Lutheran Pastoral Conference had chosen as its topic, "The Baptism in the Holy Spirit." One of the speakers was Harald Bredesen from Mt. Vernon, New York.

Pastor Bredesen talked about what had happened in his own life and in his church. He also described the move of the Spirit in the denominational churches. This was all new to most of the forty-odd Lutheran pastors attending the conference. They sat in stunned silence, and when Bredesen had finished speaking, no one raised a question.

Finally Pastor Richard Neuhaus broke the ice. "We can't just walk away from this," he protested. "These men have just made some of the most amazing statements ever heard in a Lutheran pastoral conference. Either they are liars, or they are crazy, or they are right. Either this is of God or of Satan. I don't think we can leave here until we find out."

But how to find out? That was the question. Pastor Bredesen had been a Lutheran; now he was a pastor of a Reformed church. The other pastor on the program was a Presbyterian working for his doctorate at N.Y.C. Should I give my testimony? I had determined to wait a while before telling my brethren what happened to me on December 7. As far as I knew, the only Lutheran pastor who had ever publicly testified to the Baptism in the Holy Spirit had been summarily relieved of his pastorate.

I leaned over and whispered to Harold Bredesen, "I received the Baptism a few days ago, but I was going to keep it quiet for a while. Should I give my testimony now?"

"Praise the Lord," he burst out in typical Bredesen fashion. "That's the answer. There is no other way to get the message across to these men. I'm sure this is of God. By all means, give your testimony now."

"Mr. Chairman." I stood up slowly and faced the conference with fear and trembling.

"This same thing happened to me a few days ago while I was praying alone in my church. So far, it's been all that these men say it is. I feel that a tremendous change has come into my life through the power of the Holy Spirit."

All at once, there was an explosion of questions from every side. The conference didn't know Bredesen and the other speaker, but they knew me well. The tremendous spiritual hunger in the lives of these Lutheran pastors began to come out into the open. It was decided to extend the meeting after lunch and continue the discussion as long as anyone wanted to stay.

After lunch, everyone seemed to have a hundred questions. More important, they all seemed to desire the power and the joy which had been described. The attitude of the entire group was positive. No sooner did Bredesen suggest ministry, than a number of pastors knelt at the altar rail. Others knelt in the pews and began to pray silently. Bredesen laid hands on the pastors at the altar. He began to pray over them.

Nothing happened.

I was asked to join in ministering. Still nothing happened. It must have been one of the most pregnant moments in the entire history of the Lutheran church. There was an uneasy silence. No one seemed to know what to do. Several of the pastors kneeling at the altar rail began to squirm a bit.

Abruptly, Bredesen went over to the organ and began to play soft music, apparently forgetting how thoroughly

Missouri Synod Lutherans are indoctrinated against all emotionalism. Several of the kneeling pastors jumped up and hurried back to their seats, ashamed of having exposed themselves so completely. The magic moment was gone. But a new dimension was opened up in the Lutheran church that day that would never be entirely closed again.

A new dimension was opened up in my life, too—persecution. A few days later, I was summoned to Manhattan to meet with the district president.

"What's this I hear about you and the Holy Spirit over there in Brooklyn?"

"What did you hear, sir?" I asked, stalling for time.

"That you had some kind of great religious experience and that you speak in tongues and possess all the gifts of the Spirit."

"That's an exaggeration, sir. But ever since the new '41 hymnal came out, we've been saying every Sunday, 'Oh, Lord, open Thou my lips, and my mouth shall show forth Thy praise.' The words have suddenly become real, that's all."

"Well," he said, thoughtfully, "just don't get carried away; people might not understand. What's this business about tongues anyhow? Isn't that Pentecostal?"

"Yes, sir, I suppose so, but it's also biblical."

"Hm. Well, just don't push this," admonished the president, concluding the meeting.

But I was emboldened to press just a bit further. "There is one more thing in the hymnal that we recite every Sunday, from Psalm 51."

"What's that?"

"Take not Thy Holy Spirit from me."

So ended my first hearing. To this day I do not fully understand why the Holy Spirit is such a threat to the institutional church. Perhaps what the denominational leaders really cannot bear is being out of control—the "sovereign unpredictability" of the Spirit. When God takes over His church, anything can happen.

By the middle of January, the first golden glow of the spiritual honeymoon had begun to fade a bit. Satan was running some sneaky little doubts into my mind. Had I perhaps imagined the whole thing? Was I cracking? After all, I had been working pretty hard. And then some of the Pentecostals and other charismatics I had met since December 7 did appear to be a bit on the kooky side.

Margie's reaction was a bit puzzling, too. She knew that a big change had occurred in me, and yet she didn't seem to take the whole matter too seriously. Several times, she had asked to be prayed for, but when nothing seemed to happen, she went back to life as usual. In the meantime, I stopped drinking. I also stopped spending so much money on myself. So anxious was I for Margie to share this, that often in the middle of the night I would lay hands on her silent, sleeping form and pray.

I also tried to share something with my congregation. They knew that something had happened, but they weren't sure just what. I alluded to the Spirit again and again in my preaching, but who listens to preaching? I also witnessed to a number of the members very directly. Either they didn't understand, or they seemed to take it all for granted. After all, wasn't I their pastor? I was supposed to have all the gifts of the Spirit. So, what else was new? But a few individuals did begin to show strong interest, and we formed a prayer group. The Spanish congregation seemed to grasp best what had happened. Pentecostalism was well-known to Latins. They expressed a strong desire to hear more, but my Spanish-speaking associate was very much opposed to charismatic renewal. He had apparently had some rather bad experiences with Pentecostals during his years in Cuba.

What I badly needed at this point was some kind of manifestation to convince me and others. God had to do something specific outside of me. After January 1, I began a three-week tour of duty at Lutheran Hospital. There, unknown to me, God once and for all was planning to convince me that what had happened was real.

VII

LUTHERAN HOSPITAL

I had become one of the part-time chaplains at Lutheran Hospital in Brooklyn late in 1956. I was responsible for visiting the Lutheran and other Protestant patients and also for conducting a weekly worship service over the public address system. It was a way of picking up a little additional income and also a way of sharpening my hospital ministry.

When I graduated from the seminary, I realized that the weakest points in my ministry were in the areas of youth work and hospital visitation. I was too old to do much in the youth field, but I could still learn how to do effective sick visitation and personal counseling. Lutheran Hospital, located near Brownsville, the most decayed of all the Brooklyn slums, offered a variety of pastoral experience.

In 1959 I had been a patient at Lutheran for a week, observing the chaplaincy from the patient's end. I discovered that there was a great variety of approaches to ministry to the sick. Most pastors seemed terribly self-conscious about ministering to fellow clergymen. They felt free to laugh and joke, but when it came to anything spiritual, a terrible block would develop. After the usual banter and kidding, the awkward issue of ministry invariably arose.

"Well, Erve old boy, the Lord be with you, and all that sort of thing. I suppose you can pray for yourself, ha, ha."

By this time, the visiting clergyman would begin to waltz around in obvious embarrassment. Should he pray for me or shouldn't he? What would I think about his words and style?

By this time, we both would be sweating. I wanted to be ministered to, but I also wanted to get my poor colleague off the hook.

"Oh sure, I can still pray, sick as I am. Even though I must have committed some big sin to get here, the Lord will no doubt still hear my prayers. But if you have any spare time, you can always offer up a few silent prayers for me."

"Of course. We'll all keep you in our prayers. God bless you. Good-bye."

Some of the ministers had a regular routine. One beloved brother never failed to pray for me, but he always turned away from me and faced the wall. God must have been in the corner—either that or he was facing Jerusalem. Somehow, I didn't feel included in that prayer.

One of my fellow chaplains at Lutheran had a routine that I liked very much. He would take the crucifix from around his neck and place it in my hand. Then he would pray for me while laying hands on my head, and when he said the benediction, he dipped his thumb in oil and made the sign of the cross on my forehead. I felt like I was really getting my money's worth.

I adopted his routine because I felt that he was at least

doing something. Whenever a patient was in an emergency situation, everybody rushed around doing something. Everybody except the chaplain. He just stood in the way, muttering prayers to himself and feeling useless. The Catholic priest had his confessional and his elaborate last rites. Now at least I had a crucifix, a bottle of oil, and the laying on of hands. Even though it didn't seem to do any good, I did have an identity and a function. I could always say, "Excuse me, doctors, but I think I'd better anoint the patient with oil."

"Oh, of course, chaplain, perhaps you had better. We need all the help we can get."

At the time God and I had it out, I had been a pastor for almost ten years and a hospital chaplain for seven. To the best of my knowledge, I had prayed for thousands of sick people, served communion to them, laid hands on them, and anointed them with oil. Yet nothing had ever happened.

No, that was not entirely true. There was one instance in St. Louis that did look like a direct answer to prayer. A woman about six months pregnant was seriously injured in an automobile accident. After she had spent three weeks in the hospital, the doctors concluded that the fetus had died, since there was no sign of quickening and no detectable heartbeat. Plans were made to remove the dead fetus, but the mother protested rigorously. Nevertheless, the operation was scheduled for twelve o'clock noon on Sunday. In the eleven o'clock service, we prayed for the mother. As they were wheeling her into surgery, the infant within her began to kick. The operation was called off, and two months later, a healthy child was born.

That one shook me up a bit. I talked to the doctors about

it. All they said was, "We do things, and the Man Upstairs does things. We know a little about what *we* are doing, but we don't know a thing about what *He* does. That's in your department, Rev."

Did the Man Upstairs really do such things? If so, then why so seldom? I had heard and read stories about "faith healing" and found them hard to believe. In fact, several times I had preached against the sensationalism surrounding Oral Roberts. If God still healed and performed miracles, then why wasn't anything happening in my ministry? If the age of miracles was really over, then what was all this talk about? Radio programs in the St. Louis area had been constantly advertising miracles and healing. Was it all fake?

In January of '64, when I began the tour of duty at Lutheran, I continued my former routine exactly. I did not tell anyone about December 7 but pretended to be the same old card-carrying Lutheran chaplain, which was easy, because by this time I was beginning to doubt the validity of my experience anyhow.

My very first case was that of a black opera singer from Canada. She had been scheduled for a radical colostomy— removal of the lower bowel and surgical creation of a new bowel outlet—and had refused the operation. In such cases, the chaplain was usually called in, in order to persuade the patient to follow the doctor's recommendation.

The patient's husband had apparently been told that the cancer had already begun to spread and that there was little hope that the operation would be able to remove it entirely. Nevertheless, it was her only hope, and he consented to the proposed surgery without really knowing how drastic it was.

Mrs. Gold (and that was also her color) was cheerful,

outgoing, and deeply spiritual. She was not yet fifty and wanted very badly to live. When I went in to see her, she pumped me as much as she could to get information about her condition. This was routine, since nurses were forbidden to discuss diagnosis and prognosis with patients, and doctors normally avoided doing so, if at all possible. This left only the family and the chaplain, who were lay people and not expected to understand medical terminology anyhow. The chaplains were granted access to the medical charts, and after a time, we were able to understand the most commonly used terms. I knew what a colostomy was, and the word always sent a little shudder of revulsion through me.

"Chaplain or Reverend—what do you want to be called?"

"Almost anything will do; my people usually call me Pastor."

"What do you really think my chances are?"

"Wow! That's really a hard question. I'm not a doctor, you know."

"Of course I know, but you must know something about my case. I know more than my husband and doctor think I do. This colostomy thing is pretty bad, isn't it?"

"Yes, to be honest with you, it is.

"Pastor, do you believe in the healing power of prayer? But of course you do, or you wouldn't be a chaplain, would you? I have a lot of faith, but right now it needs to be strengthened a lot. So I'm glad you've come."

Now I was really on the spot. Up to this point, I hadn't really believed in the healing power of prayer. But Mrs. Gold's faith was contagious, and suddenly I found myself believing, at least a little. We prayed my usual bedside prayer. "Lord, give Your power to the medicine, Your skill to the doctor, and Your love to all who minister to the sick. Pour out upon this, Your daughter, the power that made the blind to see, the lame to walk, that cleansed the lepers and raised the dead. Lord, You once healed all who came to You by touch, by word, and by the laying on of hands. Reach out now with that same touch and speak that same word. We thank and praise You, and by faith in advance, accept Your healing gifts and blessing. Now may the blessing of Almighty God, the Father, the Son and the Holy Spirit, be with you and strengthen and heal you. Amen."

We were both crying when I finished praying. Why was I so moved? I had taken that prayer out of the Lutheran Pocket Agenda years before, just because I happened to like it. With certain minor variations, I had prayed it so many times that one could almost hear the archangels before the heavenly throne groaning, "Oh, here comes Prange's prayer again."

So why was I crying like a baby this time, and why was I so sure in my heart that the prayer had finally gotten through?

We talked for about thirty minutes. The presence of the Lord was unmistakable. His peace and His love were so powerful that I didn't want to leave. Mrs. Gold's face and eyes were brimming over, and tears were still running down her cheeks when I left.

When I saw her the next afternoon, she was still groggy from the anesthesia, but her spirits were high. We prayed together briefly, and I left.

I saw her almost every day during the next three weeks.

Recovery was slow and painful, but steady. She was a joy and an inspiration to everyone on the floor. She was also my promoter.

"You've got to have Pastor Prange pray for you. He prays so beautifully, and I'm sure the Lord hears him."

I blushed and resolved to get some new prayers right away. Better yet, I would pray just as the Spirit might lead me.

After Mrs. Gold had been discharged from the hospital, I went to visit her in her home several times. Her colostomy was successfully reversed, and she recovered fully. Her husband then told her the following story:

"Do you remember that night before your operation when we sent for the chaplain?"

"Yes, what about it?"

"Well, the doctor told me that the cancer had already spread too far and that you had only about six weeks to live. Shortly after the operation, he called me into his office. He had a funny look on his face. 'I want to show you something,' he said. He took one of his biggest surgical knives and with all his strength burst open some small nutlike things.

" 'These are cancer seeds,' he said. 'Sometime between the examination and the operation, the cancer seeds in your wife's body became encapsulated or coated with this hard covering. They are still there, but they have been rendered harmless.' "

As far as I know, Mrs. Gold is still alive and well today.

The next case involved a member of St. Mark's congregation. Mrs. Mary Meyer was German—or rather Hungarian. Her ancestors had migrated from South Germany to the

Austro-Hungarian Empire some two hundred years before, but had retained their Germanic language and customs. They had also acquired a great deal of rich Hungarian farming land, so at the end of World War II they were expelled. Mary had migrated to America earlier and gone into the knitting-mill business in the Ridgewood section of Brooklyn.

At one time, these "Landsleute," as they were often called, formed the backbone of St. Mark's congregation. The German language was retained within the church because the generation born in Europe had never learned English. The Landsleute were fine, hard-working people, but somewhere over the centuries, they had picked up the disconcerting habit of attending church two or three times a year whether they needed it or not. On Christmas, Easter, and Good Friday, the church would be crowded; but in between, only the faithful few came. And no amount of preaching or exhortation could change this deeply rooted cultural pattern.

Mrs. Meyer was about sixty-five when she was admitted to Lutheran Hospital for examination. The diagnosis: terminal cancer. Her daughter had spoken to me the Sunday before and told me that her mother had only a few months to live.

When I walked into her room on Thursday evening, I found her very agitated. Our conversation was all in German.

"Pastor, I heard something I wasn't supposed to hear. I found out what I have. It's cancer, and it's terminal."

"How do you feel about it?"

"I want to live, of course, but I had a strange dream this

week. I dreamed that I was climbing up a mountain. It was misty, but I saw my husband at the top. You know, he died two years ago. He seemed to be stretching out his hands to me and saying, 'Come on and join me.' Then suddenly he was gone, and when the mist cleared a little, I saw the tower of a church and the carillon was playing, 'Come to church, come to church.' When I looked more closely, I saw that it was the tower and bells of St. Mark's."

I prayed for wisdom and then spoke. "You haven't been very faithful in your church attendance. The Lord is telling you that you are not ready to go. He is also telling you in very plain language to be faithful in your church attendance. Let's pray that He will give you a little more time for grace." It was the prayer of Hezekiah, the prayer for extension of life for a special purpose.

We prayed, and the glory of the Lord filled the room. That was Thursday evening. On Saturday, she was discharged from the hospital. Five years later her doctor pronounced her completely free of cancer. He said that her case was one in 200,000! Oh, yes—her church attendance improved markedly.

The next case in Lutheran Hospital involved a black woman who had come in for surgery. I checked her card—a routine pre-op—and made a routine visit.

"I'm Pastor Prange, the hospital chaplain. I think that you are scheduled for surgery tomorrow."

"Yes."

"What church do you attend?"

"Never been inside a church in my life."

"But your admission card says Protestant."

"Obviously, I'm not Jewish, and I'm not Catholic."

70

"And that makes you Protestant by default?"

"I suppose so."

"Well, anyhow, would you like me to pray with you?"

"I suppose so, if you want to."

By this time, I was beginning to feel rejected and somewhat hostile. I could sense that the patient was unusually hostile toward me. We prayed, and I laid hands on her head for the blessing. Then I walked out of the room and thought, "Well, that's that. Why don't these unchurched people just put 'no church' on their admission forms?"

The next day I just happened to be passing by the woman's room. The door was open, and she was sitting up in bed reading a book. I ducked back and looked again. It was the New Testament!

"Hey, you're sure looking chipper. Thought you'd still be conked out."

"Oh, hi, Pastor. They canceled the operation."

I started to leave.

"Not so fast! I want to talk to you."

"Yes?"

"Yesterday when you came in, you didn't mean a thing to me."

"I know."

"Your prayer didn't mean a thing either, but when you gave me the blessing, something happened. Say, how long has this book been around? I just can't put it down."

"Oh, a couple of thousand years or so."

"Well, I'm going to find out what all this is about. I feel great. Never felt better in my life."

Six months later, I saw her again—a radiant, practicing

Pentecostal. She had been healed, converted, and filled with the Spirit by a blessing, and neither one of us had had any faith! Later on, I found out that the Pentecostal church in her neighborhood had been praying for her for a long time, but they couldn't get near her. The Lord then put her in a hospital so that a Lutheran chaplain could bless her into becoming a Pentecostal!

As the time went on, there were many similar cases. Not only did I come to believe in the healing power of prayer, but my faith must have been contagious; the patients also began to believe.

The Lord had given me a clear sign, a sign from without. Whatever had happened or not happened on December 7, He was now able to use me in a completely new way. Maybe I had not changed on the outside, but inside, a brand-new channel had been opened.

VIII

A FOOL FOR CHRIST

Early in the spring of 1965, the Lutheran Women's Missionary League asked me to be the guest speaker for their international convention which was to be held at the New York Hilton in May. Over a thousand delegates, representing the congregations of the Atlantic District of the Lutheran Church, Missouri Synod, would assemble there.

It was a challenging invitation. They let me choose the topic. I wrote the program chairman that I was going to talk about "Spiritual Renewal in the Church Today." Somehow she understood, "Spiritual Renewal in the Urban Church Today." It sounded harmless enough. The inner-city church was always a favorite topic for those far removed from it.

The publicity went out all over the country. In the meantime, I had spoken about my charismatic experience at our district pastoral conference. Neither the district president nor anyone else had raised any serious objections. Everything was going very smoothly—too smoothly!

The great night came. Margie and I sat at the head table with all the VIPs, including the district president. During the excellent meal, I was still wondering exactly what I was going to say. A small voice seemed to be saying, "Give your testimony, as you did at the pastoral conference."

That sounded simple enough. As I finished my dessert, I could see the friendly faces of these Lutheran ladies turned expectantly up toward me. Most of them were in New York for the first time, and they found the experience simply overwhelming. And now, unbeknown to me, they were waiting to hear some exciting stories from inner-city ministry.

I stood up, feeling even more tense than I had that day at the conference. It still wasn't too late to back down. I could just relate some exciting stories about the church in Brooklyn. Why not tell them about the Celestians, the Mafia, the con artists and the muggings? How about telling them about integration and the trilingual ministry? Wasn't that unusual enough?

But the inner voice kept saying, "Give them your testimony. This opportunity will never come again."

"But Lord, You know these people; they won't understand. As for me, well, You know what will happen to me." But while these words and thoughts were racing through my mind, a thousand faces out there were waiting—from the whole Northeast.

"Let us pray," I began softly. We all bowed our heads, and there was silence in the huge auditorium. There may also have been silence in heaven for the space of a few seconds. "Lord, guide my words and send them forth with Your Spirit. Minister to hungry hearts and renew Your whole church. I offer up to You what will be said here tonight. Amen."

Then I gave my testimony, simply and in detail. I started with December 7 and told the whole story. The vast sea of faces took on a puzzled and then a somewhat stunned look. Faces from the podium began to glare at me, and a faint whispering could be heard throughout the banquet hall. I began to understand how Martin Luther must have felt at the Diet of Worms.

Recklessly, I plunged on deeper and deeper into ministerial disaster. I heard myself saying, "What God has done for me, He can do and wants to do for you and for the whole Lutheran church. This is not just for pastors and not just for the inner city, it's for everybody, because the promise is to you and your children!"

I sat down. The reaction was not long in coming. The district president walked over to me and said abruptly under his breath, "I wish you hadn't done that."

"Done what, sir?"

"Given your testimony in all detail."

"But, sir, I did the same thing at the pastoral conference, and you said it was perfectly okay."

"Those were pastors, and these are lay people. And women, to boot. I'm glad at least that you had the grace to qualify this as only your own opinion. Do you mind if I say something to the group about your presentation?"

"Not at all, sir."

Meanwhile, there was great commotion in the assembly. The president of the LWML was turning alternately purple and green and then white, as she choked for words. Down on the floor, women were asking each other, "What did he say? What did he mean?"

Advisory pastors were running around trying to straighten

the delegates out. The district president stood up and repudiated my testimony. He said, in effect, that the implication that God was real was my own personal opinion and did not necessarily reflect the official doctrinal position of the Lutheran Church-Missouri Synod.

Actually, a heartening number of delegates understood exactly what I had said and were trying to explain to the others. The rest of the program was forgotten as the women broke up into excited knots of discussion.

We had come with the Krauses. I grabbed Margie, George, and Helen, and we fled the wreckage of the 1965 LWML Convention. I felt that I had made an utter fool of myself and would never live this down. On the way home in the car, there was a protracted silence. George tried a few corny jokes, but they fell flat.

Finally I said, "Well, I guess that does it. That's the last time I'm ever going to give my testimony. In fact, that's the last time I'm ever going to even talk about the charismatic renewal. From now on, if anyone wants to know anything about God, let him find out for himself. I've had it! This finishes my career in the Lutheran church."

The others tried to encourage me. "It wasn't that bad, Erve. In fact, it was quite good. The only problem was that it's all so new to those gals. Anything goes here in New York, but in the rest of the country they get shook up easily, especially Missouri Synod Lutherans. They'll get over it, and so will you."

They tried hard, but I felt terrible for about three days. I might have felt worse except for the fact that we had received a three months' leave of absence to go to Guatemala where I would serve a trilingual congregation. We planned to drive all the way in our new Chevie wagon.

In the excitement over the trip, I began to forget about the New York Hilton. But the women of the LWML didn't. I received a surprising number of encouraging letters and a few questioning ones. A group of Lutheran women on Long Island had even signed a paper supporting me and censuring the district president for repudiating my testimony. In the ensuing years, I would come across little renewal cells all over the country born out of that night when I was willing to be a fool for Christ. The husband of one woman returned from the Air Force as a major and entered the seminary at Springfield. He started a charismatic cell at Springfield that now numbers about thirty-five students.

The drive from New York to Guatemala was quite an adventure. The thing that hit us, both in Mexico and Guatemala, was the unbelievable poverty. Crossing the Rio Grande River from Texas to Mexico was like entering another age. The people and the language on the border were more or less the same, the land and climate were the same, but the standard of living was centuries apart. What made the big difference, industrial organization or the blessing of God?

The poverty in Guatemala was, if anything, worse than the poverty in Mexico. The average Guatemalan Indian family lived on the United States equivalent of about seventy dollars per year. Everywhere we stopped in Mexico or Guatemala, hordes of dirty, ragged little boys descended upon us and wanted to do everything from shining our shoes to shining the car. In Guatemala, the cry went up everytime we parked anywhere, *"Cuida su auto?"* (Watch your car?). This usually meant that they would protect the car from themselves.

In Guatemala, our station wagon represented the life income of about seven Indian families. The expensive German camera I was carrying would have supported an Indian family for about six years. How would it be possible to communicate the Gospel across this tremendous economic gap?

Antigua is one of the most beautiful cities in the world, in spite of the fact that it has lain in ruins since 1773 when a severe earthquake leveled the city, destroying some eighty magnificent churches and monasteries, some with stone walls eight-feet thick. The ruins are still pretty much the same as they were on that fatal day. At one time the Spanish capital of America, Antigua lies at an altitude of 5,000 feet and is surrounded by nine volcanoes, one of which is still somewhat active. The climate is almost perfect and has earned Guatemala the title of "Land of Eternal Spring." Flowers of every description bloom profusely throughout the entire year.

After the earthquake, the capital was moved from Antigua to Guatemala City about thirty-five miles away. I served a trilingual church in Guatemala City and also attended the University of San Carlos. We lived at the Lutheran Hour compound in Antigua, and every day, I drove to Guatemala City across a 9,000-foot pass.

The country was in a state of revolution. Martial law had been declared. Every day, the sentries at Antigua and

Guatemala City noted the time of my coming and going as well as the number of my passengers.

In spite of the poverty and the revolution, I loved lush, breathtaking Guatemala. To me, the climate and the scenery were like paradise compared to Brooklyn. And so, when the congregation in Guatemala City gave me a call, I wanted to stay.

Around and around the Lutheran Hour compound I paced. It was a glorious day. The coffee plantations all around were a rich green; every kind of tropical flower was in glorious bloom. The air was crystal clear and just the right temperature. There couldn't have been a more perfect day since the dawn of creation. I felt that I could almost reach out and touch the distant volcanoes ascending up as high as fifteen thousand feet. They were all old friends by now, Agua was our nearest neighbor and Fuego was still smoking and sending up sparks on a dark night. There was Tolimán and Santo Tomás nestling over beautiful Lake Atitlán. How could I possibly leave paradise?

I remembered the first time we had visited Lake Atitlán. We stopped by the famous city of Chichicastenango where ancient pagan and medieval Roman Catholic worship took place in the same cathedral. The Indian market fair was in full swing. On the steps of the cathedral, witch doctors were busy with their incantations; inside, corn and other grain was being offered up to pagan gods. Every Sunday, a Roman Catholic Mass was celebrated in the same church.

Lake Atitlán is no doubt the most beautiful lake in the whole world. The water stays at about 72 degrees throughout the entire year. In some places, the bottom has never been measured. The water is very clear but shimmers in

iridescent colors when the breeze blows. Magnificent volcanoes stand like giant sentinels guarding the whole scene.
Their blue cones ringed with white clouds are constantly
reflected in the mirror of water. One morning the T. L.
Osborne Evangelistic Mission brought truckloads of Indians
in their brilliant native costumes, and hundreds were
baptized in the lake. If I could live any place in the whole
world that I wanted to, it would be on the shores of Lake
Atitlán in Guatemala.

How could we possibly leave Antigua? There was the
Posada de Belén or the Inn of Bethlehem where we all went
for a brief swim every day. The gardens of this resort inn
must look like Eden did before the Fall. The inn was
founded as a hospital by Hermano Pedro, a Spanish
nobleman turned Catholic lay brother. The cruel conquista-
dores exploited the Indians terribly in the name of the
church. One day Brother Pedro began to care for the sick
natives. This one life of selfless love transformed the rather
sordid history of Antigua. In the midst of cathedrals and
monasteries destroyed by the wrath of God, the Posada de
Belén, a monument to the love of God, remained.

On that perfect day of Eternal Spring, God and I had it
out once more.

"Lord, can't I stay here?" I pleaded. "You know You
need a trilingual Lutheran preacher here. I've started Bible
classes and prayer groups, and I intend to do a lot more as
soon as I finish this term at the University. Please, God!"

"No." It was not thunder or earthquake, nor the rumble
of a volcano, but a still small voice deep within.

"But why? I've put in my time in the ghetto. It's so
beautiful here, and so ugly in Brooklyn. After all, You made

all this beauty. I can worship You a lot more easily here than I can among the garbage cans. Nature itself is Your cathedral here. Look at the clouds supported by the mighty volcanic cones; Solomon's temple was nothing compared to this!"

Go back to the city and die.

"But what about Margie and the children?"

When I call a man, I call him to die.

"Yes, Lord."

IX

CARLITOS

Shortly after we returned from Guatemala, I went to Bogotá, Colombia, to conduct a retreat on charismatic renewal for United States and native pastors. The night before I left Bogotá, I was invited to hold a prayer meeting in the home of the president of the Colombia District of the Lutheran church.

Besides Pastor and Mrs. Morck, another Lutheran pastor and his wife were present. Our special guests were three Mennonite missionaries working in Colombia. One of them was a woman in her early forties who had been working in an orphanage in Bogotá for eight years. She approached me toward the end of the meeting.

"Pastor Prange, I have colitis. It's getting worse. The doctors say there is no cure and that I must give up my work very soon. Do you believe that this is God's will?"

"No."

"Do you believe that God wants me to give up my mission work?"

"No."

"Do you believe that God wants to heal me?"

"Yes."

"Then what are we waiting for?"

We prayed for her with the laying on of hands. The next day I flew back to Brooklyn and heard no more about her, but about a year later I received a letter from a Mennonite pastor in Medicine Hat, Alberta. He said that she was a classmate of his at the seminary and had been totally and instantly healed of colitis that night in Bogotá, Colombia. He wrote because he suffered from the same disease and wanted me to come out and pray for him, too.

Divine healing often works just like that. Countless thousands of cases must go completely unreported. Many are still obeying the command of Jesus, "Go and tell no man."

Very often, divine healing takes place when there is no other possibility. It is closely related to human faith which may be stimulated by utter desperation or effective witness. Most dramatic healings which take place are, in my opinion, sign healings meant to be a witness to the fact that even though we walk by faith, God is still among us performing His mighty acts.

Such was the healing of Carlitos. Carlitos, or "Little Charlie," was a bright and handsome Puerto Rican boy. He was only four months old when his father was killed in Vietnam. Nellie, his mother, and Carmen, his grandmother, attended St. Mark's Spanish service. Nellie was a licensed practical nurse who worked in a physician's office. For some time, she had suspected that Carlitos might be a "hemophiliac," a bleeder. She kept her suspicions to herself, but she began to run laboratory tests on the clotting factors in her son's blood.

One day when he was about a year old, Carlitos fell and cut his mouth badly. His mother tried to stem the bleeding but couldn't. She took him to the doctor for whom she worked. He, also, was unable to stop the bleeding and advised Carlitos' mother to have him hospitalized immediately. Up to this point, neither of them had mentioned the dread word "hemophilia."

For two days and one night, Carlitos continued to bleed. One Thursday night, Nellie brought him to the prayer meeting at church. No one said anything to me about the problem. However, when he began to bleed copiously, I had one of the men rush him and his mother to the emergency room of Lutheran Hospital.

The intern and the nurse on duty in the emergency room tried for some thirty minutes to stem the bleeding. All of their best efforts only made it worse. When the intern found out that Nellie was a nurse, he said, "Look, let's face it: he's a bleeder. There is nothing more we can do. He will have to be hospitalized immediately."

By this time Nellie had become panicky. She was afraid that if she left Carlitos in the hospital, he might never come out again. She had lost her husband; she wasn't going to give up her son.

In the meantime, the prayer meeting at the church had been concluded, and part of the group had gone to the home of a young Spanish couple who lived nearby, where we continued the prayer meeting in Spanish.

We were praying in Spanish when Nellie walked in with

Carlitos in her arms. He had been vomiting blood, and both he and his mother were soaked in blood from head to foot. Nellie held up her son and moaned, *"Que vamos a hacer, ahora?"* (What do we do now?)

Lisa, our hostess, turned to me and said, "Why don't we pray for him?"

We walked up to Carlitos, laid our hands on his bloody head, and began to pray. Lisa prayed in Spanish, and I prayed in English. "Lord, heal Carlitos, now. In the name of Jesus, stop the bleeding."

Suddenly, as if someone had turned off a faucet, the bleeding stopped. Carlitos jumped out of his mother's arms and began playing on the floor as if nothing had ever happened. We all looked at him, expecting to see the rug stained with blood. There was no fresh blood to be seen. Carlitos had been limp and pale. In front of our eyes, his face and body seemed to change. He began to laugh and jabber in Spanish and English. We looked at each other. No one spoke. We were afraid to believe. Finally, Lisa whispered, "He's been healed. I know it." I wanted to believe, but I knew how easy it was to jump to conclusions. I also knew that hemophilia was incurable. After a short prayer, the meeting broke up, and we all went home, wondering what we had witnessed.

The next morning, when Nellie woke Carlitos, there was no sign of blood. She opened his mouth and looked inside. There was a long white scar like that of a wound several months old. That day she took him to her doctor for an examination. The doctor had seen Carlitos shortly after he had begun to bleed. Now he, too, carefully examined the scar for some time in silence.

Finally he spoke excitedly. "It's a beautiful job. Whoever sewed him up performed a work of art. You can't even see the needle holes. I was afraid to suture the cut, because I knew he was a hemophiliac. I knew that every time I stuck the needle in, the bleeding would only get worse. Who sewed him up anyhow, and how did he stop the bleeding?"

"Dios." (God.)

"Dr. Dios? I've never heard of him, which hospital is he with?"

Nellie then told him the whole story, but he stubbornly refused to believe. For six months, Nellie did regular checks on the clotting factors in Carlitos' blood. Everything appeared to be perfectly normal. There was no evidence of hemophilia. She carefully gathered together the results of the tests she had been conducting for some time before the bleeding episode. One day she laid the entire file on the doctor's desk. He paged through it quickly and then closed the file. Nellie was peering over his shoulder.

"What do you think now, Doctor? You know there is no real remission in hemophilia, but this certainly looks like one, doesn't it?"

"I refuse to look," he said. "If I did, I might have to change my entire theory of medicine, and that I'm not prepared to do. Let's wait and see; I'm sure that he will bleed again."

But he didn't. The years have passed, and Carlitos' blood has remained perfectly normal. However, Carlitos has never been the same again. Something else happened that night when he was prayed for—something deeply spiritual. If it is possible for a little child, Carlitos was baptized in the Holy

Spirit the night he was healed. His experience has had a profound impact upon the entire family.

It was Carlitos who brought his grandfather to the Lord, shortly before the grandfather was killed in an automobile accident. It was he who brought the family to church every Sunday. He had his mother and grandparents conduct family devotions every evening. Many times he woke Nellie up in the middle of the night so that they could pray together. Carlitos was not a "tither," he was a "hundred percenter." Whatever money he happened to have with him—ten cents or ten dollars—went into the collection plate.

Carlitos had lost a father, and his grandfather was killed before he was three. He decided that I would have to serve as a substitute. He told everyone that I was his father, and every time he saw me, he would jump into my arms and hug me as hard as he could. Sometimes, during the Spanish service, he would come into the sanctuary and give me a hug. He insisted on coming to communion and could never understand why I wouldn't give him the wafer and the wine.

Carlitos has seen all the pain and evil that life in the inner city can concoct. But God has put a special mark upon him. In the midst of it all, he walks in serene spirituality and at the same time is totally a boy. He says that he is going to be a minister, and I'm sure that he will.

That night in Lisa's apartment, the Lord healed a boy and called a disciple.

X

HARVARD AND THE BLUMHARDTS

In the fall of '66, I received a Merrill Fellowship to Harvard Divinity School. I took a leave of absence from St. Mark's for one semester and moved into the Divinity School dormitory. The family stayed behind in Brooklyn, and every other weekend, I drove to New York.

The fellowship was both generous and flexible. I was more or less turned loose in Harvard. I soon realized that in the Divinity School library alone, there were more books than I could read in several lifetimes. I began to wander through the stacks like a homeless ghost. I had to focus on something, and very soon decided to zero in on divine healing.

There was a wealth of material, but how was I going to narrow it down? I read the Christian Science material, the stories of the Roman Catholic apparitions, such as Lourdes and Fatima, and I even began to read some of the psychic research of Oliver Lodge and others. None of these sources gave me what I was actually looking for. I wanted concrete evidence in church history of divine healing as a gift of the Holy Spirit.

Divine healing had cropped up again and again in the church. Every time there was some kind of spiritual renewal, there were also reported healings. The Holy Spirit and physical healing appeared to go hand in hand, although in classical Roman Catholicism, the Virgin Mary and the saints almost replaced the Holy Spirit. Sometimes healing was associated with some rather questionable movements, and perhaps for this reason, the mainstream of the church had tended to shy away from the subject entirely.

What I needed was solid Lutheran evidence. But where? I had a complete set of Luther's works at home and knew that there was very little from Luther directly. The church historian, Sauer, usually reliable, said that Luther possessed all the gifts of the Spirit, including tongues. But that statement stood alone without further documentation. Luther did pray for Melanchthon at one time when he was seriously ill, and Melanchthon recovered immediately. Luther also wrote a famous letter of instructions for praying for the sick. Outside of these references, there seemed to be nothing. Not even enough about which to write a short paper.

Because of the fanatical "Enthusiasts" of his day, such as Storch, Schwenkfeld, Muenster and others, Luther apparently took a rather dim view of the manifestations of the Spirit. There are many directions that the Reformation could have taken. It could have become experiential or institutional; for better or for worse, it chose to take the doctrinal route.

Day and night I haunted the stacks of the Divinity School library. By now I knew what I was looking for—an authentic Lutheran link to the manifestations of the Spirit. But where, who?

One night I was on the lowest basement level. It was late and eerily silent. The dust on the books indicated that they were seldom disturbed from their rest. Everything was new and fascinating to me, but a kind of mysterious anointing coupled with unusual anticipation guided me down a particular row in a dark corner of the sub-basement.

What an accumulation of human thought and experience surrounded me! Row upon row of theology reached from the floor to the ceiling. Several of the ancient tomes represented the life work of a dedicated saint. Now they lay here, forgotten and untouched. Here was the experience of the church waiting to be sifted—a modern valley of dry bones.

Could these bones live? They were once a mighty army, men of faith marching through history, living and dying. They once were ideas and hopes and dreams—must they rest forever in the dust of neglect?

"Son of Man, prophesy to the bones." I breathed a fervent prayer for guidance. Out of the blurred mass a name emerged: *Blumhardt*. Somewhere I recalled having heard the name before, and here they were, more than three dozen volumes, all in German, telling in detail about a Lutheran-Reformed charismatic renewal in Germany during the eighteen hundreds. And the spark to the whole thing had been divine healing. Here was the "pearl of great price," the "treasure hidden in the field," that I had been almost unknowingly searching for.

Time stood still. This was the eternal moment before God, although the library clock struck one, two, three, and then four in the morning. To me, it was like the discovery of the Pacific or the deciphering of the Rosetta Stone.

Johann Christoph Blumhardt lived from 1805 to 1880, and his son Christoph from 1842 to 1919. The elder Blumhardt was educated for the Reformed ministry and became pastor in Moetlingen, a small village in Southern Germany. I remembered visiting Moetlingen many times during my stay in Germany after World War II. The town was clean and quaint, but hardly exceptional.

Blumhardt's career was relatively uneventful until in 1842 one of his parishioners, a girl named Gottlieben Dittus, was diagnosed as being demon-possessed. At first, Blumhardt refused to take on the case. Doctor after doctor was called in, until finally one of them came to Pastor Blumhardt and asked pointedly, "Are there no Christians in the village?"

Blumhardt got the point and reluctantly undertook the battle. Besides the strange nervous disorder suffered by Gottlieben, there were numerous psychic phenomena in her home observed by the rest of the family as well as many villagers. When Blumhardt began the battle, he prayed with Gottlieben, "Lord Jesus, help us. We have watched long enough what the devil does. Now we want to see what You can do."

Thus was joined a tremendous spiritual battle that continued for almost two years. Sometimes Blumhardt and Gottlieben recited together the verse from Luther's "A Mighty Fortress Is Our God"—"Though devils all the world should fill, we tremble not, we fear no ill, they shall not overpower us."

The battle went on. Blumhardt refused to give up, even

though the situation seemed to be getting worse rather than better. His parish work was being neglected. He was getting very tense and very tired. The whole village was watching, and word was beginning to spread to the outside world. As the onlookers watched the exhausted pastor, they wondered if his strength—or faith—would fail him before his mind gave way. Which it surely had to, for the pressure was building unbearably. Almost constantly now, Blumhardt was prevailing upon the Lord for more grace. Yet even as his stamina ebbed, his determination seemed to grow stronger.

Suddenly one day, the crisis came. Gottlieben's sister, who was in the room, gave a long rattling cry in a strange voice—*"Jesus ist Sieger"* (Jesus is victor)—and it was all over. That day, many people in the village reported hearing the whirring of wings plus despairing cries, *"In den Abgrund, in den Abgrund, weh, oh, weh, wir muessen in den Abgrund!"* (Into the abyss, into the abyss, woe oh woe, we must go into the abyss!)

"Jesus is victor," became the battle-cry of Blumhardt. The victory over the demons that bound Gottlieben led to a breaking in of Kingdom power which transformed the entire village. There was renewal beyond Blumhardt's wildest dreams. Lives were transformed, marriages were saved, enemies were reconciled, and there was an outpouring of witness and testimony.

Most of all, there were healings. Almost every time Pastor Blumhardt laid hands on one of his members for absolution, a healing took place. There was a new depth in his preaching as well, and people came from all over Germany to hear him. He conducted five services each Sunday, and the little church was filled to capacity each time with people sometimes standing as far as a kilometer away. One Sunday, the German emperor himself came to see what all the fuss was about.

Inevitably, the jealousy of Blumhardt's colleagues began to cause pressure to be brought to bear on him. He left his parish and founded the healing center of Bad Boll in Württemberg.

Christoph Blumhardt was born in 1842, the year in which Gottlieben Dittus was delivered. He followed in the footsteps of his father, and in the 1880s was renowned as a faith healer and evangelist. In the early part of the twentieth century, he was elected to the German parliament on the Socialist ticket. He is credited with discovering the social dimension of the Gospel, and his theology had a profound influence on Dietrich Bonhoeffer.

Both Blumhardts lie buried at Bad Boll, which is still flourishing. I smiled to realize that I had walked past their graves several times with no idea who they were.

The Blumhardts were both solid, unflappable characters. There was nothing of the fanatic in them. Men like Karl Barth, Emil Brunner, Paul Tillich, and Oscar Cullman numbered them among the great theologians of the nineteenth century. The real mystery is why they are so little known in this country, and why they were so soon forgotten.

The two main thrusts of the Blumhardt theology are very relevant today. "Jesus is victor" was their battle cry, and "the Kingdom" was their theme. They taught that Jesus was victor—once and for all—on the cross some two thousand years ago, and that He will be victor again when He comes with all His power and glory at the end of this age. But He

93

is also victor now, as the Kingdom breaks into our brokenness and sin. The Kingdom is not only something past and future but a real, active alternative in this present world.

This is a charismatic theology. It is easy to believe that Jesus once was victor in the remote shadows of history. It is also easy to believe that He will be victor again sometime in the dim and distant future. To believe that He is victor right now over disease, indifference, and evil takes a slightly different kind of faith. The question, "Are the manifestations of the Spirit for our time?" is also the question, "Is the Kingdom for our time, or is it only past and future?"

The other Blumhardt theme is that of brokenness. Here, the Blumhardts are very close to Watchman Nee. Their theology is not the Reformed emphasis on the Old Testament covenant of prosperity and blessing, but the New Testament theology of the Cross. Christoph Blumhardt quit at the height of his fame and success in Berlin in 1888. He believed that the renewal came not through success and triumphalism, but through brokenness and humility.

There are increasing signs today that the "New Renewal" or the "Renewal of the Renewal" is going to follow this demanding path. As Watchman Nee says in *The Release of the Spirit*, "The Spirit can only be released after both body and soul are broken." The alabaster box and the grain of wheat must be broken and die before the new life of the Spirit is released.

The question of Christoph Blumhardt still rings in the churches' ears, "Whose cause are you seeking, your own or God's?" Both liberals and Evangelicals have a lot to learn from the Blumhardt story and the Blumhardt theology. It seems likely at this point, as we stand at the crossroads of renewal, that the greatest hour of the forgotten Blumhardts is yet to come.

There has been a thread of renewal running through all of church history, but most of it has been lost, distorted, or discredited. The Blumhardt story is different. Here are many volumes of solid renewal theology, untainted by scandal or fanaticism—a mountain of gold waiting to be mined.

The Blumhardt story taught me one very important lesson. Standing between the church and renewal is the tremendous but secret power of the enemy. Once that is overcome, the Kingdom can break in. But this takes God-given courage and perseverance. The "strong man" is not going to be defeated by weak faith. We are in a battle. The first thing we have to do is put on the whole armor of God and then carry the attack to the enemy. All the spiritual weapons offered us in Ephesians 5 are weapons for attack. The armor is for our front. If we turn our backs on him, we are lost.

I came back from Harvard with a certainty that Jesus was victor. That victory was soon to be tested. I also believed that the Kingdom was breaking into my own life, but didn't know yet that the Kingdom comes only through brokenness.

XI

THE OCCULT

When I returned from Harvard just before Christmas of '66, there were a few problems awaiting me. First of all, my trilingual associate was planning to leave, and all attempts to find a replacement for him proved futile. This meant there would be no more luxuriant leaves of absence, and I would be preaching in German, English, and Spanish every Sunday.

To make matters worse, I enrolled in the graduate schools of New York Seminary and the Postgraduate Center for Mental Health. In the spring, my application for another chaplaincy was processed, and I was appointed Protestant chaplain of Greenpoint Hospital in Brooklyn.

All at once, I was putting in a hundred hours per week, working for the Lord—but I was too busy to pray or study the Word. Life became a series of hectic emergencies and impossible schedules. It actually got so ridiculous, that at one point, I was supposed to be in four different places at the same time.

I became a total stranger to my family. Sunday afternoon, after conducting services in three languages, I would closet myself in the upstairs bedroom and sleep for three hours before the Sunday night hospital calls and services. Some weeks, I visited as many as five hundred hospital patients in addition to my regular parish duties and a twelve-hour study load in graduate school. It was absolutely insane and becoming clear to me that my exaggerated idea of my own self-importance had gotten me into this mess, but seeing that did not show me how I could extricate myself.

All the while, the enemy was carefully preparing his strategy. When I was utterly depleted, physically, mentally, and spiritually, he intended to sift me like wheat. His opening gambit came early in February '67.

One day the telephone erupted in a volcano of Puerto Rican Spanish. Spanish verbs and adjectives poured out of the earpiece like white-hot lava. Nouns and prepositions seemed to chase each other up and down the cord. Margie shook the receiver violently, but it didn't seem to help. I tried shouting, *"Mas despacio, por favor!"* (More slowly, please!) When Puerto Ricans get excited, they all speak in tongues, and only God can understand.

Finally, I began to understand. The caller, a woman named Lucia, was trying to tell me that her sister was possessed by a demon, and that I should come at once. On the way, I picked up Maria, another Puerto Rican woman, and the three of us rushed to the Bronx where Lucia's sister lived.

When we arrived, the police and an ambulance were already on the scene. The apartment was a nightmare. Everything breakable, including all the windows, had been shattered. Broken dishes, splinters of furniture, and shreds of cloth created a scene of demonic devastation. In the midst of the destruction stood a hefty young Puerto Rican girl clad in a straitjacket and a torn dress. Three hospital orderlies were struggling with her. Two policemen were looking on, wondering exactly what to do.

When we entered, there was a pause. Lucia's sister, Juanita, recognized me.

"Pastor, ayudame, ayuadame!" (Pastor, help me, help me!) Then another voice, deep and menacing, came out of the same throat. "Stay away from me, you dirty priest, or I'll kill you."

Classical schizophrenia manifested this kind of split personality, but schizophrenics did not usually go berserk. Even though this was my first personal experience with demon-possession, I knew it could be nothing else. I remembered, then, that Lucia had told me that her sister often attended spiritualistic séances.

At the hospital, Juanita, her husband, and I were taken to one of the waiting rooms in the emergency clinic. A huge, red-haired policeman guarded the open doorway. Lucia and Maria stood just beyond the policeman. Outside in the main hallway, almost a hundred people awaited admission to the emergency clinic. It was not an especially good place for exorcism.

Nevertheless, I began. I addressed the demons in English, Spanish, German. "In the name of Jésus, and by the power of His blood, I command you to depart. Satan, I come against you and your host in the name of the Lord. Out, foul, unclean spirits, in Jesus' name!"

The policeman began to look at me strangely. He assumed I was a Catholic priest, and so I threw in a little Latin for his benefit. But the demons weren't fooled. They knew they were dealing with a somewhat frightened amateur. I remembered what happened to the sons of Sceva: "Jesus I know, and Paul and I know, but who are you?"

A voice from somewhere inside the stricken girl began to taunt me. "I am Lucifer, the prince of spirits, and you are a mere mortal. You cannot cast me out."

"I can't, but Jesus can, and I am His servant and speak in His name."

"Even Jesus called me the 'prince of this world.' "

"You are lying—you are just some minor demon. What is your real name?"

"I am Juanita's father."

"Her father is still alive. Come out of her, you lying imposter!"

"I'll show you who I am, Pastor Prange. Let me remind you of a few interesting episodes from your own past. Do you remember back in Germany during the war? The night in Speyer, when you drank all the brandy and then got on the table and made a speech? Do you remember that young Polish girl?"

"Shut up."

"Oh, there is a lot more I could tell. Do you want to hear it?"

The demon was speaking in Spanish, and the voice was getting louder and louder. The Puerto Ricans waiting outside were beginning to listen. I wasn't sure that I understood everything, so I went to the door and checked with Maria.

"Pastor, he's telling your whole life history."

But how could he know? How could anyone know? Was

he reading my mind and memories? I asked the policeman if Maria could come in and help me interpret. He nodded, fascinated by the whole drama.

We both began to pray, and Maria laid hands on Juanita. In her perfect Spanish, she commanded the demon to be silent and depart. I began to pray loudly to cover up my own uncertainty.

"All right, I'll go. But I'm going to get you two for this. I know a way. I know something you don't. You're both going to become very ill. And something even worse is going to happen to you. Just wait and see. You've got a lot of nerve going around casting out demons and healing the sick. You do it only because I let you."

"Liar!" I shouted in English. "Go. Leave instantly. Be bound and be cast into the abyss. Jesus is victor! Jesus is victor!"

Suddenly there was silence. Juanita sat up as if nothing had happened. She was perfectly calm. Half an hour later, she was discharged from the hospital, and Lucia, Maria, and I drove back to Brooklyn.

Lucia told me that Juanita started out as a Catholic in Puerto Rico, then became a Jehovah's Witness and finally a Spiritualist. She had been attending séances several times week. I remembered reading somewhere that more than a third of the Puerto Ricans in New York had dabbled in spiritualism at one time or other.

I was strangely uneasy. In Harvard, I had come across the writings of William James, Oliver Lodge, and Arthur Conan Doyle. They had conducted extensive scientific investigations into the whole field of the psychic about the time of World War I. Was there a direct connection between the occult and the demonic, or was this just primitive superstition?

Juanita's demon had been real. There could be no doubt about that. What about the threats? Surely a demon didn't have this much power over believers. Nevertheless, cold, dark forebodings rose up within me.

A month later, Maria and I were both hospitalized. I had bleeding ulcers, and she underwent major surgery and almost died. Coincidence? Superstitious fear like a voodoo spell? These things just didn't happen in the twentieth century. Or did they? In the meantime, the enemy was preparing his real attack.

St. Mark's prayer and healing service was held every Thursday night in the church, and anyone could and did walk in. It was a perfect setup for infiltration, and I was a perfect target for the intellectual and sophisticated forms of the occult.

It began with Helga. She was a lovely, intensely spiritual woman, if at times a bit absentminded and vague. She had spent some eighteen years in India and had lived in an ashram and studied under a guru. Through it all, Helga remained a devout and deeply committed Christian, although she was not affiliated with any particular church.

Through Helga I met the assistant Indian ambassador to the United Nations, as well as several prominent swamis. She could tell fascinating stories about the mysticism of India.

Whenever her guru needed anything, he would simply snap his fingers and it would materialize right out of the air. She showed me a very valuable solid gold crucifix he had given her as a going-away present. The guru just snapped his fingers and there it was! Sometimes her guru would cook beans and rice in a little black iron pot. Thousands of hungry people would line up to be fed, and the pot would not be empty until everyone was satisfied. According to Helga, her guru could leave his body anytime he wished and travel anywhere in the spirit.

We didn't quite know what to make of Helga's stories, but she was a wonderfully spiritual person, and meditating with her was always an experience. She would sing a little song or chant and call the angels. At the time, Helga was almost seventy, but when we were praying in the dimly lit church, she sometimes seemed to be as young as twenty. Whenever she was around, one was aware of a powerful spiritual presence. At no time was there ever even a hint of the demonic.

Through Helga, the subject of reincarnation was introduced into the group. Sometimes she would vaguely hint that she had once been an angel but had volunteered for a human incarnation in order to be able to relate to God like the redeemed. Sometimes I even felt that she might have been an angel sent to me. Whenever I needed her, I would simply project the thought, and a few minutes later the phone would ring.

"Yes, Pastor, how can I help you?"

Helga was no kook, and she was one of the most loving individuals I have ever met. She literally spent her life doing good—yet—she was one of the subtle channels through which the occult began to influence my life and thinking.

Jack was another. He, too, was a very spiritual person and worked full time for world peace. Through him I had complete access to the United Nations and to many very prominent people. As it happened, Jack was a good friend of Bishop Pike and his son. Our prayer group was aware of young Pike's problem and had been praying for him. The night that Pike's son killed himself, I couldn't sleep for some reason and spent several hours in the church praying. At 3:00 A.M. I knew that it was all over and went back to bed. Several other members of the prayer group had had similar experiences that night.

Through Jack we were introduced to the cult of Edgar Cayce and also to several members of Spiritual Frontiers. These did not immediately become issues of any importance, but the seed had been sown.

And now, little things began to go wrong. People left the Thursday night prayer group. Dissension came. I couldn't understand what was happening. The anointing seemed to have been removed.

I started a second prayer group in Spanish. It met on Monday nights. Although the group was small, the power and the blessing returned. Something was definitely wrong in the Thursday night group.

The entire issue was complicated by the indisputable fact that St. Mark's Church and parsonage were haunted. From the day that we first moved in, there had been tappings in the walls, voices, and other manifestations. Lights were turned on and off, the shower and the TV would often be turned on full blast by unseen agents. We called the ghost "Oscar" and made jokes about him, but Oscar was all too real.

When we first moved to Brooklyn in 1956, Margie and I slept just above my office. Night after night there would be a terrific disturbance in the empty office. I could hear chairs being moved around and cabinet and desk drawers being slammed. But every time I ran down boldly or stole down quietly, there was nobody there. Going through old records, I had found an intimate personal diary. I hid it away for future reference. The diary disappeared, and the disturbances stopped.

Several years later, our daughter, Diane, slept in the bedroom above the office. Several times she woke us in the middle of the night with her screams. We would find her under the bed or under the mattress in a state of near shock.

"What's wrong, Diane?"

"I heard these footsteps coming up the stairs, and I thought it was one of you. I looked out into the lighted hallway, but when the steps got to the top, there was nobody there, and I just screamed. I know I heard them, and I know I was awake."

Once Diane was studying in the living room directly across from my office. Through a mirror on the wall she could see directly into my library. I was in the church when I heard a piercing scream. Right away I thought of burglars and came running through the door between the parsonage and the church. Diane was shaking like a leaf.

"I saw someone taking the books down off the shelves and looking through them. I thought it was you, but when I called, no one answered. I went to look and there wasn't anyone there. But someone or something was taking books down off the shelves."

"Which books?" I asked. She showed me. They were all books about the occult.

Several weeks earlier, Pastor Kraus had called and asked if I wanted some books. One of his members had died and left a house full of books, and the landlady wanted to get rid of them. I came and loaded up my station wagon with about a thousand volumes. Most of them were on science, but quite a few dealt with psychic research and occult phenomena. I placed the occult books on the top shelf of my library, hoping that I would find time to glance through them some day.

In the meantime, my mother came from Texas and spent several weeks with us. She stayed in Diane's room. On the way to the airport for the trip back to Texas, she suddenly blurted out, "Erwin, I didn't want to say anything, but there is something wrong with Diane's room."

"What do you mean exactly?"

"Sometimes, about 3:00 A.M., I would wake up and hear tapping noises in the wall next to the church. Sometimes I would hear moaning and crying coming from within the church."

"Why didn't you say something before?"

"I was afraid. And besides, I don't believe in ghosts. You ought to know that."

"You still don't believe in ghosts?"

"I just don't know what to think."

I didn't know what to think either. Oscar was getting out of hand. One night I was sleeping alone in the bedroom above the office. At 3:00 A.M. I woke suddenly to find a roomful of gray faces staring at me. Was I dreaming? I shouted, "Get out of here!" and they vanished. About a week later, it happened again. This time I asked, "What do you want?" Like some tragic Greek chorus, they chanted in unison, "Pray for us, pray for us."

Was it a dream or was it real? I wasn't quite sure. I

mentioned this in a prayer meeting when someone from Spiritual Frontiers happened to be present.

"Oh," he said, repeating what I was later to learn was one of the most popular occult cons of all. "Those are earth-bound spirits who used to belong to this church. They are stuck on the astral plane and need your prayers." The fact was, they were demonic spirits, masquerading as lost souls, but I was woefully ignorant of the wiles of Satan. I had no idea what in the world those words were supposed to mean, and I was afraid to ask.

XII

BUSHWICK PARISH

In February of '64 I had attended my first International Convention of the Full Gospel Business Men, at Washington, D. C. The whole thing was new and exciting. Everyone was so friendly and so hungry for the Word. I gave my testimony before the largest crowd I had ever addressed in my entire life.

The next morning was International Youth Morning. Young people from all over the world and from every denomination had come together to share the Lord. This was really new for a Missouri Synod Lutheran who wasn't even allowed to fellowship with Lutherans of other synods.

These young people seemed to be having a great time in the Lord. The room was filled with joy, love, and praise. Once more the Lord seemed to be clearly speaking to me. *You must work for the unity of the church, no matter what it costs you.*

"But Lord, why pick on me? You know very well how my church body feels about ecumenicity. Why don't You get yourself a liberal Methodist or Congregationalist, or better yet a Universalist? Why must You always get me into trouble?"

Back in Brooklyn, His words continued to haunt me. Bushwick had once been known as the "Avenue of Churches." Looking North from Pennsylvania Avenue, one could see steeples row on row. I was always a little proud that St. Mark's steeple towered over the others and dominated the whole scene. It almost seemed to be standing in the middle of Bushwick Avenue, keeping all the rest of the churches in line. It stood on a slight curve and was framed by the Myrtle Avenue El.

But not even St. Mark's could prevent the inevitable decay of Bushwick Avenue. Many of the steeples it supervised were silent monuments of better days and were perched rather precariously on the top of ruined and empty religious mausoleums. Unity of doctrine wasn't nearly as hard to achieve as unity of color and race. As Bedford-Stuyvesant began to spill over Broadway into Bushwick, the white residents fled to suburbia, leaving their beloved churches behind them.

The Catholics and the storefronts stayed, plus St. Mark's and a few others. The Roman Catholic concept of the geographical parish made it natural for them to stay, and the storefronts catered to the new residents, whom they exploited as well as helped. The Protestant concept that your church is where your people are made it easy for them to rationalize abandoning the inner city and fleeing to suburbia.

Those who stayed realized they could no longer afford the luxury of extreme denominational competition. It was stand or fall together. We also realized that if we were to relate to the community in any kind of meaningful way, it had to be together. The community was fragmented and divided enough without the church adding to it. For too long the people of the city had witnessed the scandal of a divided church.

A meeting of Bushwick area pastors and priests was called to discuss our common problems and goals. For want of a better name, we called ourselves "Bushwick Parish." In the New Testament, the church had been the church in the place, such as the church at Ephesus or Corinth. We were simply the church at Bushwick—Catholic and Protestant, black, white and brown.

The main question: what could we do together? We had to keep the horizontal and the vertical dimensions of the cross in balance. The horizontal pointed out toward man and helping our brothers, and the vertical pointed up to God and following His lead. How could we be totally God-centered and relevant at the same time? Everybody had a different plan, but praise God, the hand of the Spirit was upon us, shaping, guiding, and inspiring.

We finally organized into various task forces to deal with certain common religious and community problems. I was elected to be in the Clergy-Police-Community task force.

That story began on Labor Day, 1967. Usually when everyone else fled the city, we stayed to enjoy it. New York traffic on work days is bad enough, but on holidays is simply unbelievable. I have spent as long as four hours in the sweltering sun crossing the eight miles of Manhattan, thinking that I could almost push my car that fast. New York drivers are not pokes; there are simply too many cars for a given space.

The same was true of the beaches. Wave-to-wave people with a few bare spots of sand showing between was just too much of a good thing. So we stayed home in our postage-stamp backyard to enjoy the relative peace and quiet—until the phone rang. An excited female voice with a slight Spanish accent was shouting, "There's a riot! The street is full of police and people. The riot squad has come. Dick went out to help, and now the police are beating him. They are arresting him and taking him away in the paddy wagon. He was painting my apartment. His wife isn't here, my husband isn't here. Pastor, you've got to come right now and stop them. They can't arrest Dick!"

It was a big order. The street was only two blocks away, but by the time I got there, Dick was gone and his wife had returned. She was in hysterics, and people were milling all over the street. Black Panthers were already on the scene, threatening to put snipers on the rooftops and shoot it out with the police. I tried to calm everybody down, but they were all shouting, in three languages.

I drove with Ann, Dick's wife, to the nearest precinct. On the way, she filled me in on the details. She knew the patrolman who had arrested Dick very well. Once she had written a letter to the mayor about the police, and they had threatened her. In turn, she had chided them for shaking people down for money. At that time, she said what years later was openly alleged: that many New York City policemen were taking graft.

The riot had supposedly started when two patrolmen from the local precinct tried to shake down a black Puerto Rican who had two arrests for car theft. An argument ensued, and as a result, the Puerto Rican and his family were allegedly beaten. A crowd began to gather, and Dick, who had seen the whole thing from the apartment window he was painting, tried to help.

Dick was a painter by profession. He was also a Spirit-filled ex-alcoholic, kind of a hero on his block and in his church. Dick spent all of his spare time witnessing and helping others. He would go down in the Bowery and pick up hopeless drunks, dry them out, and try to steer them toward rehabilitation. He also worked with AA and Boy Scout groups in the church. He was the nearest thing to a real live saint that Bushwick Parish had.

When Ann and I got down to the precinct, we asked for Dick and were told that he had already been taken down to police headquarters at Schermerhorn Street. Later on, we learned that while they were talking to us, Dick was upstairs being beaten unmercifully. The lieutenant at the desk asked me if I wanted to fill out a civilian complaint form. I said that I certainly did and filled out the form to be processed through the civilian review board.

All day long we looked for Dick. Finally at 9:00 P.M. we found him at the Schermerhorn police station. By this time we had collected a lawyer and a lot of witnesses.

When Richard finally walked into the courtroom with hands cuffed behind him, my heart skipped a few beats. He looked as if he had tangled with a bulldozer. His eyes were half shut, and his face was bruised and swollen. He walked with a limp, and there was matted blood on his head. Only the crown of thorns was missing. I was afraid to look at his hands. He stood there with his eyes downcast and uttered not a word. My eyes filled with tears, and a lump came into my throat. The words came first in Latin as I thought of the famous painting, *"Ecce Homo"* (Behold the Man). Christ before Pilate. This is how it must have been. The Word keeps on happening.

We bailed him out and took him home. On the way he told his story. All the time they were beating him at the precinct, he was praying, "Father, forgive them, for they know not what they do."

"This will teach your wife not to write letters to the mayor criticizing the police." With that, a 230-pound patrolman hit him full in the face with all his might.

"Father, forgive them." *Pow*, right in the teeth!

"You must be some kind of religious nut," they said, panting. *Pow! Pow!*

"I love you, and God loves you, too." *Pow!*

"I'll show you what love means," the policeman said through clenched teeth, and hit Dick with all his might. Finally, Dick fell into the merciful silence of unconsciousness.

Afterward, "Blackie," the Puerto Rican whose shake-down had started the whole riot, was beaten. Richard tried to interfere and was beaten again. He got down on his knees and began to pray in his cell. The police were baffled. They could deal with threats, curses, and violence, but not with prayer.

There was an investigation, but it turned out to be a whitewash. Then Richard and I told our stories over the radio, and I began to be persecuted. The president of the Patrolmen's Benevolent Association of NYC singled me out as being "anti-police." I began to feel depressed. How could I possibly function with 24,000 patrolmen on my neck? I laid my problem before a large prayer group in New Haven,

Connecticut. Immediately, people began to pray for me. The next day, an inspector of police appeared in my office. He was Jewish.

"I want to help you," he said.

"Thank you, Inspector. I could use a friend or two right now."

He did help, and together we worked out a plan for Police-Clergy-Community cooperation which is still in effect.

God used this incident to bring about some badly needed reforms. The prayer of the ex-alcoholic being beaten in his cell, "Father, forgive them," was not without fruit. This is the most powerful prayer we can pray, because it plugs right into the cross. It draws on the very power that redeems us.

The story of Bushwick Parish is not complete. But God's Spirit is working where human need is the greatest. Too often, when the church tries to become relevant, it becomes secularized and drifts into humanism. The experience with Dick taught me that everything the church does must begin with Christ as its head. Too often we come up with what we think is a great program. We ask the Spirit to bless it, but He says, "It wasn't My idea in the first place. Why didn't you ask Me in the beginning?" Relevance begins with God.

XIII

MONTANA

Early in 1969, a letter arrived from Libby, Montana. It was from Art Neils, a member of St. John Lutheran Church in Libby. He, his wife, Jean, and some of his relatives had become involved in spiritual renewal in 1965 when a charismatic revival swept through the little lumbering and mining town in northwestern Montana.

Art informed me that their incumbent pastor was planning to resign because of ill health. Don Pfotenhauer had given him my name. Art wanted to know whether I might possibly be interested in a call to Montana in the fall.

That's the kind of question to which a Lutheran pastor can never give a completely frank answer. All he can really say is, "If I should receive the call, I will certainly give it my sincere and prayerful consideration." But I was interested. The pressures of Brooklyn were getting both me and the family down. We needed a change of pace and a breather after thirteen years in the New York ghetto.

Art and I continued to correspond and also spent considerable time and money on the telephone. In October, the pastor at St. John in Libby did resign, and the call process began. The first three men called declined, and by this time, I was ready to remove my name from the call list. However, during the holiday week between Christmas and New Year's, Art and Jean invited Margie and me to be their guests in order to look over the Northwest. It was slightly irregular according to Missouri Synod Lutheran practices, but we decided to go, avoiding the members of St. John, if at all possible.

The flight from Kennedy to Spokane was nonstop and short. As soon as we got out of the East, our tensions began to ease. The flight across the snow-covered continental divide was indeed out of this world. Even at 39,000 feet, we felt that we could almost reach down and touch those incredible Rocky Mountains.

Art and Jean met us at the Spokane, Washington, airport. They were very gracious, and their faces shone with the joy of the Holy Spirit. Pastor Erwin Sprengler and his wife joined the four of us for dinner. The Sprenglers had recently received the Baptism in the Holy Spirit, and although we didn't know it then, Pastor Sprengler was about to lose his parish because of controversy over the gifts of the Spirit. He and I hit it off right away, perhaps because all men named Erwin are immediately joined together in a bond of mutual sympathy.

The difference between Spokane and New York was simply too great to be spanned in a mere five hours of flight. In the history of this country, it was a difference of almost three hundred years. All around us were symbols of the frontier and of the great American West. Since the American frontier was as recent as my own boyhood in Arkansas and Texas, I experienced a strange sense of nostalgia. In spite of all those years in the East, I was still a Westerner at heart.

On the drive from Spokane to Libby, I also realized that in spite of all the years in the city, I was still just a country boy. The stillness of the snow-covered landscape was almost unbelievable after the continuous din of New York City. It was almost as if we had landed by mistake on some strange silent planet. The beauty of the rugged mountains that surrounded us on every side was almost too much. There was hardly any traffic and very few towns. Once in a while, a sudden clearing and a lonely cabin would surprise us when we rounded a mountain curve. We almost felt like intruders.

Libby was an attractive little town nestling in a high valley with the Kootenai River on one side and the beautiful Cabinet Mountains on the other. The highest of the Cabinets was less than 9,000 feet, but they seemed much higher since they sprang straight up out of the plateau. Because Libby lies sheltered in a high valley, the wind blows right over the top of it and the snow falls straight down, sometimes piling as high as eight feet on the level. The winter before we came, the temperature dipped to fifty-three below zero at the Libby ranger station, but they say it felt like only forty below, if that is any comfort.

The chief industry in Libby was the old J.J. Neils Lumber Company purchased by the St. Regis Paper Co. in 1957. The giant dam, spanning the Kootenai River upstream from Libby, was in the process of being built. Scheduled for completion in 1975, this dam was to create a lake some 130 miles long, reaching deep into Canada and impounding over 7 million acre feet of water.

We were impressed by St. John Church and school, and even though we had not intended to, we met a few of Art's friends and relatives at his home. It was December 30, the weather was warm and sunny, and a beautiful blanket of snow covered all the imperfections of Libby's rather poor streets. It looked and felt like home. The people of Libby seemed like our kind of people, whatever that means.

Back in Spokane, I had a speaking engagement with Pastor Sprengler. Thirty minutes before the meeting was scheduled to begin, we had no meeting place! Suddenly the Lord provided, and we ended up with about 120 people. I was scheduled to talk about the Trinity and the inner city, but somehow we ended up talking about spiritual renewal. Afterward I said to Pastor Sprengler, "You take the Holy Spirit line, and I'll take the healing line." Neither he nor anyone else seemed to know what I was talking about. We all gathered around a large table, held hands, and began to pray. Even though I hadn't anticipated it, a number of people received the infilling of the Spirit that night.

After the meeting, Margie and I caught a train for Seattle. We had a sleeping compartment, and the station and everything else was right out of the last century. I couldn't sleep, but lay awake, feeling the train sway and listening to the engines chug and blow across the mountains.

After visiting relatives in Tacoma, we went back to Seattle and attended a meeting at Dennis Bennett's Episcopal church where I was scheduled as one of the minor speakers for the evening. I was tremendously impressed at the smooth organization and obvious success of St. Luke's in spite of the fact that Dennis was seldom there. He always seemed to be off on some trip. Surely this had to be of the Lord, because the part that man played was less than obvious.

When we landed at Kennedy in New York, I began to feel the oppression again. Because of a tailwind, the flight from Seattle had lasted only four hours, but it took almost two hours to find our baggage, get to the car, and fight our way home through the traffic. It wasn't good to be back in New York, even though we were glad to see the children again. I prayed, "Lord, let this be the last time that I land here to stay."

Early in January, 1970, the call to Libby came, and I really faced the thought of leaving St. Mark's. We had been there almost fourteen years, and in spite of the tensions and difficulties, our roots had sunk deep. When I shared the call with the congregation, at first there was silence and then consternation. They couldn't believe that I would leave them after all those years. It had taken a long time to gain the confidence of the blacks and the Latins. It had been a long time before the neighborhood admitted that I existed. Was I prepared to give it all up? New York, with all the problems, also presented great opportunity. How could I bury all that experience out in the lonely, cold mountains of Montana?

The agony of decision was real and deep. I was the one who finally had to decide. What was the Lord saying to me? I drove to a retreat center in New Hampshire to meditate and pray. Every inner voice and every sign said, "Go. Now is the time. Your work here is finished." My family said the same thing. But I wanted to escape so badly, how could I trust my own judgment?

The hour finally came. I announced my plans. The farewell service was a joint service of all three language groups. We communed from the common cup as usual. Black, white, brown, German, Irish, and Italian mingled salty tears with the blood of Christ. If I had left at any other time, it wouldn't have been this way. I knew it was time to go.

On March 17, 1970, we arrived in Libby, Montana. Our furniture was already there, set up in the parsonage. I moved into my new forty-thousand dollar office, put my feet on the desk, and admired the fantastic view. "I will lift up mine eyes to the hills, from whence cometh my help." With these words of Psalm 121, the Spirit welcomed me to Libby.

Libby was a chance to catch my breath and a chance for me to get acquainted with my family again. I went hunting and fishing with the boys whenever I had the chance. Yet adjustment to a small town was far more difficult than I had dreamed.

Among other things, my work-week was suddenly cut in half, and I had time to read again. What did I read? The books on the occult that had been given to me. There were a number of books on reincarnation plus scientific reports about contacts with the dead. I found the subject tremendously fascinating. All of the time, I quieted my uneasy conscience by saying, "This is scientific and spiritual research." I had read severe Christian warnings against the occult but had dismissed them as Fundamentalist propaganda. The books written against the occult did not begin to match the sophistication of those written by Sir Oliver Lodge, Flammarion, Frederick F. W. Meyers, and other scientists who had devoted themselves to psychic research.

The worst part of it was that I began talking to people about psychic things, and when there were repercussions, I was amazed and hurt. I would even make up my mind not to talk about it anymore, and almost against my will would find myself blurting out something.

There was a renewal cell in St. John and quite a number in Libby, but there was also controversy and opposition. I played it cool. There were some healings, but we didn't advertise them too much.

On June 20, 1970, I was called to Kalispell, Montana, to visit an ex-pilot who had suffered a severe heart attack. When I arrived, the cardiologist had just brought in the X rays and the EKGs. "Russ, let's face it," he said to the patient. "Two-thirds of your heart has been destroyed; you'll be an invalid the rest of your life." The day before, Russ had suffered a massive heart attack right in the hospital. His heart had stopped for several minutes.

Russ told me about it, and he also told me about an experience he had had. When his heart stopped, he saw himself lying on the bed and realized that he wasn't in his body. He walked outdoors. Kalispell was even more beautiful than usual in June. The cherry blossoms had an ethereal quality about them. The weather was perfect, and the mighty mountains of the Continental Divide looked as if they reached to heaven. Suddenly he came to a checkpoint. A high spiritual being stopped him. "You must go back," he said. "Your work is not finished. A man will come, and you will be healed." The next thing he knew, he was in his own body again, lying in his hospital bed.

After he had told his story, I asked, "How's your faith now?" "Infinite," he replied. "Well, God's power and grace are also infinite," I told him. "Let's see what happens when three infinites get together." We prayed, and the peace of God filled the room.

That afternoon Russ left the hospital, and the next morning he mowed the huge lawn on his ranch. In the days following, he dashed about Kalispell like a teenager. Some months later, he spent some forty hours on a fire line. His doctor steadfastly refused to give him another examination. Finally he put in a claim for his disability insurance. The claims adjuster examined all the medical records and said, "Everything seems to be in order but one thing—you seem to be awfully healthy. Do you mind if we examine you again?" That was exactly what Russ wanted. The examination showed a perfect heart. No damage.

In January of '71 the call came from the inner city of Baltimore. I flew down to survey the situation. I took one look at the abandoned, vandalized community center, and the little storefront black church, and my heart sank into my shoes. All the people I met seemed to be very nice, however.

Back in Montana, the battle with myself began again. The boys and I often went in fishing on the beautiful Double N Lake at the foot of the Cabinet mountains. The fishing was not only excellent but the scenery was breathtaking. Even at fifteen below zero, we enjoyed it.

Just as in Guatemala my greatest personal battle took place at the foot of beautiful Volcano Agua, so here in Montana a battle took place at the foot of Mount Snowy.

"Lord, why do I have to leave here? It's so beautiful, even if it is a bit cold. And I can feel Your presence here whenever I lift my eyes to the hills."

Go back to the city and die.

It was the same still small voice of God.

"But Lord I've already done my tour of duty in the city. Almost fourteen years. Do You know how good the fishing is here? Why, the boys and I caught eighteen beautiful rainbow trout in one afternoon. And there are deer tracks all over the snow. Did You ever see so many Canadian geese in one place? Nearly every day I see a bear. The scenery is healing my soul."

Go back to the city and die! When God calls a man, He calls him to die!

"Yes, Lord."

I made plans to leave on the Sunday after Easter. On Wednesday of Holy Week, a family came through on the way to Spokane. They had a thirteen-year-old girl in a wheelchair. Her name was Crystal Lake, and her spine had been almost severed by a bullet two years before. Surgeons had placed iron rods in her back, and she had stayed in a full body cast in Shriner's Hospital in Spokane for eleven months. Her case had received wide publicity—President Nixon had written her a letter, and Vice President Agnew had visited her in the hospital and signed her plaster cast.

Now the rods were slipping, and Crystal might have to go through the whole ordeal again. She was still paralyzed from the waist down, but at least she could be at home and not be in a plaster cast. We wheeled her down in front of the altar. Margie's kindergarten class happened to be in church. At first they stared in innocent wonder and then joined us in prayer. Before the prayer, I asked Crystal's family, "Just what do you want God to do? What do you expect Him to do?" "We just don't want her to go through this rod and cast thing again," they said. "As your faith, so be it," I answered.

On Good Friday, the Lakes came back through Libby on their way to their home in Havre, four hundred miles away. Crystal was with them, and they were all beaming. The Lord had answered our prayer and also given us a bonus—Crystal was beginning to get a little feeling and movement in her legs!

Somehow I was led to say, "In a year, Crystal will be standing beside her wheelchair, walking with canes. Someday she will walk and run again." A year after we had been in Baltimore, a member of our prayer group said, "I read in the paper about a girl named Crystal Lake from Montana. She was standing beside a wheelchair, walking with canes. The headline said it was a miracle." Mrs. Perry, the member of our prayer group who reported this, had never heard of Crystal before that day.

So ended the Montana interlude. I still correspond with Art and Jean. The seed had been planted in another place, and my heart had been touched by God's beauty. I have a strong feeling that I will see Montana someday again. It was New York to Baltimore round about by way of Montana, hard on furniture, but a necessary detour.

XIV

"BILL"

His cleft, strong chin and deep voice easily made you forget that he was only five feet seven and too short to be a Texan. Behind that charming manner and magnetic smile, a brilliant mind lay hidden. When he spoke on any subject, people listened. No one who ever met him could forget Bill, especially the girls.

I first met him Christmas 1949. He had boarded with my mother while he did his seminary internship at Cisco the previous year. Mother never stopped talking about what a great preacher he was, and I couldn't help feeling a little jealous, because I knew how badly she had once wanted me to be a minister.

Bill called my mother "Grandma," and he was visiting her when we met. He was the one who talked me into going to the St. Louis seminary rather than the one in Springfield, Illinois. When I arrived in St. Louis in the fall of 1950, Bill was the only person on campus whom I knew. He took me under his wing, and we soon became good friends.

After graduation, we were both called to parishes in the St. Louis area, and our friendship continued. On Mondays we would take the day off and often went for long walks along the Missouri River. Sometimes our conversations were quite deep, but they were always about intellectual and philosophical things and not about the things of the Spirit. We were both searching earnestly for something we did not know. In our deepest moods, sometimes over a frosty stein of beer, we both knew that somewhere over the rainbow there was a real realm of Spirit.

Then I received the call to Brooklyn, and Bill received a call to Oakland, California, his hometown. During the years that followed, I saw him only once, when he came to New York to be interviewed for a position. During the night he spent with us, our parsonage and church were robbed, so he decided to stay in California where it was safe. I had also received a call to the San Francisco area but decided to turn it down.

Except for an occasional letter, there was very little communication between us. In the meantime, he had received a scholarship for a Ph.D. in clinical psychology at the University of Minnesota. Bill had been very successful in his parish in California, but he knew now for sure that something was missing. He decided that the way to the Spirit was through psychology.

In September of 1965, I received a letter from Bill, postmarked Minneapolis. One paragraph read,

> Which brings me to the burning issue—the Spirit! Both surprise and awe were my reactions to the news of your religious experiences which first reached me via Bill Puder and Walter Bouman. As you can probably guess, I am curious. What are the changes you speak about in your writings on the subject? Are you the same old Prange? Or would you say a

deep-seated personality change has taken place in you? If so, I'm not so sure I like the project. I heard somewhere that you express strong positive attitudes towards synodical programs these days. Is that true? If I hear next that you have taken to substituting milk and water for beer and Scotch, I know I'll be agin it. Seriously, I'm not about to deny the possibilities of charismatic gifts in the church, since to do so would be to deny the experiences of the primitive ecclesia. I do wonder, however, just what it is that you mean when you say in your Christmas letter that the laying on of hands has accomplished what could not be done through years of preaching and teaching. What do you mean in concrete terms?

As a result of his letter, I sent Bill a number of books on charismatic renewal plus a number of tapes. Among the books were *The Cross and the Switchblade* and *Run Baby Run*. As a psychologist, Bill worked in the field of behavior modification. These were dramatic stories of behavior modification by the Holy Spirit. I also sent him tapes by Dennis Bennett, Howard Ervin, Harald Bredesen, and Leonard Evans. He read the books, but confessed recently that he did not listen to the tapes until after he had received the Baptism in the Spirit some six years later! After I had sent the books, the following letter arrived:

I had a long letter all written to you, most of which dealt with reactions prior to my having read the books you sent. I had not received them. Before I could get it mailed, the books arrived, outdating the letter. So I had to throw it away. I must write to thank you for the shipment. I have read a good deal by now. It is not possible to react adequately to this material intellectually. If I even try to describe my emotions while reading some of it, I am sure you would not believe me. Suffice it to say, that I find most of it "moving," which strikes me as a

curious and inappropriate comment, but I will have to trust
that you understand what I am talking about. I really don't
adequately understand my own reaction.

In 1969, I attended a charismatic conference in Minneapolis, and Bill and I had a chance to renew our old
friendship. He was quite interested in the conference and
even came forward for ministry, but his intellectual reservations were far too great. In a letter dated July 21, 1969, he
wrote:

> I think one of the things I need is Spirit-Baptism, but when
> the brethren have tried to administer the Spirit to me, nothing
> happens. Don's diagnosis is that I have a demon, maybe more
> than one, but efforts to expel this demon have not been very
> successful. Besides, I am becoming somewhat skeptical about
> this diagnosis, since I hear it so frequently applied to people
> who do not appear clinically to resemble scriptural descriptions
> of the possessed.

While we were in Montana, I flew across the country
several times and usually stopped in at Minneapolis to
spend a little time with Bill. By this time he had received his
Ph.D. degree from the University of Minnesota and was
a certified clinical psychologist practicing at General
Hospital in Minneapolis.

In March, 1970, the telephone rang at 1:30 A.M. Montana
time. It was Bill. It was obvious he had been drinking.

"God loves you, but He hates me."

"How can you say that?"

"He hears your prayers and gives you His Spirit, but He
never does anything for me. You're Jacob, but I'm Esau—
red, hairy, and ugly. I'm ole no good Esau, God hated me
even before I was born."

"Now wait a minute, that's blasphemy."

"Look at what He's doing. I've prayed and you've prayed and Don's whole church has prayed, but nothing happens. Everybody else gets the Spirit except hairy ole Esau."

"People all over the world are praying for you right now."

"It won't do any good. Tell them to stop. I'm a hopeless case. If something doesn't happen pretty soon, I'm going to give up on all religion. It's just a crock, anyhow."

"Do you think you'll be any happier when you give it up?"

"Happy? Who's happy? I'm miserable. You don't know how miserable I am. No wonder Esau went hunting so much. He was trying to forget that God hated him. It's a wonder he didn't shoot himself. Sometimes I stare at my gun and wonder why I bother."

"You are supposed to be a psychologist."

"And you're supposed to be a minister, and you can't even minister to me. You won't even listen to me, and I'm paying for this phone call."

"Why do you want the Spirit so badly, and why do you keep on blaming me? Contrary to your opinion, I'm not Jacob, and I didn't steal your blessing."

"I need the power to witness naturally and beautifully. I'm supposed to be a minister, too, but I can't even witness to my patients when they say, 'Dr. Backus, we've come to you because you are a minister as well as a psychologist.'"

"Why can't you witness? You've written some beautiful things."

"I can't witness because I've never seen God do anything. I have nothing to witness to. I don't know Him personally—how can I recommend Him to others?" And so the conversation went for over two hours from Minneapolis to Libby, Montana.

In May, I drove through Minneapolis on my way to Baltimore. This time I stayed four days. For some reason, the Lord kept sending me back. He wasn't going to give up on Esau. I'm going to let Bill describe in his own words what happened.

My friend Erve Prange began traveling back and forth through the Twin Cities on his way to one place after another, and each time he would stay with me. I didn't realize then as I do now that this was all of the Lord. We would sit up late and talk and inevitably the talk would come back to the question of why I hadn't received the Holy Spirit. I learned a lot then, the hard way. It was not God who was withholding His good gifts, but it was me refusing to take the gifts. My defenses were up: pride, fear of letting everything go to God, fear of failure, and some remaining feeling that I had some precious riches that He might take away from me and that I didn't want to let go. Under such an arrangement, there was no way to realize or walk in God's perfect freedom. I was maintaining that I was a slave and insisting on keeping the contingencies in force when God has set me free.

But I kept talking. Until at last on Erve's last visit, we were talking in my living room—again about the same subject—and I had despaired of ever receiving the Baptism. All of a sudden, in mid-sentence, I stopped talking. It was as if I had come to the end of words. As if there was nothing more to say, nothing in my speech centers at all. Then I started to sob; not whimper or weep—sob—large, loud sobs and tears. I didn't feel sad particularily, just empty. The feeling was like I imagine death feels. Of coming to the end of everything: every resource, every device of self-help, everything. God was really showing me that I was poor in spirit—totally destitute in spirit, as a matter of fact. I don't know how long the sobbing continued and the sense of being dead, but when it stopped, Erve prayed for me and gave me some words to pray (I didn't have any of my own). I asked for the Baptism in the Spirit. And suddenly it came. I heard myself talking a new language—one I hadn't learned at prep school or the seminary. A beautiful new language, and I didn't have to think about it. It just flowed. And with it came the joy! There is no describing this joy! I had never known joy before. I had known happiness, but this wasn't happiness. This was the joy which is the fruit of the Spirit. I couldn't find ways to express it.

I just went on talking my new language. But that wasn't enough. The charge of energy was like a million volts of electricity looking for motors to turn and dark streets to light up like day. I threw furniture into the air and shouted. I felt justified and righteous—never felt that before. I knew it, but I hadn't felt it. I looked at the things around me: the bricks on the fireplace all looked new; each one looked perfect, and each was a window through which God poured. I ran to the door and threw it open. Outside the creation literally sang the praises of God. Every leaf, every blade of grass, had a look of perfection—was a window through which the glory of God shone. "The heavens declare the glory of God," I said, fulfilling the prophetic vision of Psalm 19, given me two years before. I had forgotten the prophecy altogether until one of the elders reminded me of it after I told him about the experience.

I ran and got a Bible and started reading it aloud. The words had flesh on them! The Word was really made flesh! I had understood them before through my training and by faith; now they were describing living experience to me—vivid, living experience. And the primary fact of life came clear; God is real. He is so real and Jesus Christ is so alive and active that anything else I called reality is a shadowy imitation by comparison. There is no life or light or reality except as a reflection of His. And the joy continued. All day, all night. That night I kept waking up and checking to see if I still had the Holy Spirit—the way a newlywed wakes up and checks to see if the beloved is really there, still there.

130

And the Lord didn't let me sleep much; in fact, since I received the Spirit, sleep is one thing there isn't much of. Many things happened in quick succession. I was healed of chronic high blood pressure which I had had for more than twenty-five years. A new and unexpected healing of the slipped disk in my spine seems to have taken place. A vigor and energy I haven't known before have been given.

As soon as I could, I took an MMPI (Minnesota Multiphasic Personality Inventory). Now some people think that psychologists fake these tests when they take them, but they don't ordinarily do that. I didn't, and I had taken the MMPI frequently before. My profiles had never been horribly malignant, but the previous MMPI had shown some rather poor frustration tolerance together with chronic anxiety and guilt. Not the one in the Spirit. Defensiveness dropped, anxiety was virtually zero; the profile I now had is that which every psychologist longs for and seldom obtains. A really comfortable, uncomplicated, non-anxious, guiltless person. And that is exactly how I felt. The profile of a person who has really been set free from bondage!

Bill is practicing psychology and witnessing. Psychology is in the business of modifying human behavior. He has demonstrated again and again that the Holy Spirit is the greatest modifier of human behavior. This has been measured and demonstrated again and again, and it is something which his scientific colleagues recognize and respect. In fact, the Spirit is working so powerfully in his clinical practice that his calendar is seldom full. Again and again his patients are healed or delivered by the Lord and do not need to come back. He uses the extra time witnessing to various professional groups.

The Lord had sent me to Montana for many reasons. Perhaps the primary one was to protect me from myself.

Certainly another reason was to minister to Bill Backus. After Bill was converted, he ministered to me when no other human could.

Shortly before I went to Montana, a student from Valparaiso University had a vision about my call. He saw a man sitting before a window holding an empty cup. I thought it was Art Neils, my friend in Montana, but maybe it was Bill instead.

XV

BALTIMORE

In May of 1969, while we were still in Brooklyn, I spoke at
the Full Gospel meeting at the Harvest House in Baltimore.
Some three hundred people were present that night, many
of them Lutherans. I spoke about prayer, using the Book of
James as my Scripture.

After speaking for over an hour, I asked if there were any
questions. Way in the back of the crowded room, a
forty-year-old man struggled to his feet with great difficulty.
He was wearing heavy braces, and he used two canes for
support.

"Pastor Prange, I've been crippled from polio for twelve
years. Have you ever heard of anyone in my condition being
healed by prayer?"

My heart sank. After I had presented such a beautiful
case for healing, why did the Lord have to test it with the
most difficult case there?

"I've heard of it, but I've never seen it nor had any part
in such a healing. All I can say is, God can do anything.
Come to the prayer line and see what He has for you."

I really didn't feel that confident at the moment. In the

confusion, I completely forgot the altar call. Everything was going wrong. This stupid Lutheran didn't even know how a Full Gospel meeting was supposed to be conducted.

The meeting had begun in a strange way, too. There wasn't any other room available for private prayer, so the chapter officers had taken me into the men's rest room. There they laid hands on me and began to pray. Catching a glimpse of myself in the mirror above the sink, I groaned in the spirit. "Lord, the things You make me do!"

I learned later that the polio victim, Bob Kline, hadn't wanted to come to the meeting in the first place. His wife and friends had practically forced him. He tried to bring something along to read but couldn't find a thing when his wife was ready to leave.

Bob was a lapsed Roman Catholic who had gotten very bitter and profane about his condition. He had been a Marine for a number of years, and after he was out of the service, polio struck. He spent two years in the hospital and some additional time in Warm Springs, Georgia. At one point, the doctors had said that he would never walk again, but then they managed to contrive an elaborate system of braces that permitted him to move about with great difficulty. At night, when Bob took off his braces and steel corset to take a bath, he crawled on his stomach like a snake in order to reach his bed.

That night at the Harvest House, Bob sat as far back as he could and tried not to listen to me. He had heard too many boring preachers and too much empty talk about healing. But somehow it seemed that every word I spoke was directed right at him. That's why he had stood to ask me the question. That's why he was compelled to join the healing line.

Three years later, in his testimony at the Dundalk Full Gospel meeting, Bob Kline said, "When Pastor Prange laid hands on me, it felt like his hands went all the way through me. It was like someone reaching into a pickle jar to fish out that last pickle. Something had been taken out of me. I went to the drinking fountain and drank two glasses of water to fill the vacuum."

The next morning, Bob had feeling in his left leg for the first time in twelve years. It began in his toes and went all the way up to his hip. He was working as a bookkeeper at St. Mary's Seminary. That day while he was alone in his office, a voice said, "Take the brace off your right leg." He looked all around but could see no one. The voice spoke again, louder and more insistent. He still paid no attention, Finally, the voice spoke a third time, this time as commanding and forceful as a marine drill sergeant: "Take the brace off your right leg!" Bob began to answer back. "I can't do it here, now. What will everyone think? Maybe they'll think I've been faking all these years just to get their sympathy."

After work that night, in the alley back of the seminary, Bob took off the brace. He drove his car without a brace for the first time since he had become crippled.

Several weeks later, the same scene was repeated. This time the voice said, "Take the brace off your other leg." This was his worst leg; it was almost totally shrunken. He was afraid and confused. On the way home, he consulted a Pentecostal neighbor who advised him to obey immediately. Bob didn't even wait until he got inside his own house. In the alley outside, he took off the heavy brace and his body corset and tossed them aside. With that, he walked into his house as if nothing had happened. At first, his wife didn't even notice.

Today Bob's braces and canes are hanging on the walls of the Gospel Tabernacle in Baltimore, where Bob is a very active member. He is learning to ski and roller-skate. Bob Kline's physical healing was also accompanied by a miraculous psychological and spiritual healing. His testimony has brought many to the Lord. It has also stimulated the faith of others so that they too could be healed. To me, it was a sign that the Lord wanted me to come to Baltimore. When I visited Baltimore after the call came in February of '71, Ed Thate arranged a meeting and brought Bob along as a surprise. It was the first time I had seen him since he had been healed. When we embraced, the thought ran through my head, "Lord, how can You do such mighty works through a miserable sinner like me?"

When I left Montana and came to Baltimore, I had continued to read in the area of the occult, and gradually, a profound and malignant depression settled over me. I blamed Baltimore and the new challenges which confronted me. Nothing seemed to work out the way I had planned. Every door I tried was either firmly closed or led to nowhere. And soon the depression turned into oppression and bondage. I could no longer sleep at night. Life suddenly became an agonizing, unbroken pain. I longed for death. What had happened? Where were the joy and peace of the Spirit?

My compulsion to talk about the psychic had already caused considerable repercussions in the Lutheran prayer groups in Baltimore. There were confrontations. I became angry and felt betrayed. I felt at first that the whole group were just a bunch of hypocritical gossips.

Just at this time Bill Backus came to Baltimore to speak at a Full Gospel chapter. He knew nothing about what had been going on in my life. When I met him at Friendship Airport, he said, "I have an urgent word for you from the Lord. It came to me on the plane, and I know it is of Him."

"What is it?" I asked, though in my heart I already knew.

"You are to have nothing more to do whatsoever with the psychic or the occult. Burn all your books and never mention it again. Moreover, you are not to let anyone talk about it in your presence. Someday the Lord may use you to warn others, but now you need confession and deep ministry."

As soon as we got to the house, I made a full confession and received absolution. I burned every book in my library even remotely connected with the psychic, and after brief ministry, the oppressive spirits left me. Never in my life had I experienced such a sense of relief and cleanness. It was like a second honeymoon of the Spirit. Later on, I was to learn through Watchman Nee's great book, *The Spiritual Man*, just how subtly Satan could gain ground in the Christian life. My deliverance came through confession and absolution. Besides gaining freedom from oppression, I also lost all interest in psychic things.

Recently the Lord has used me to speak to various groups in order to warn them about the danger of the occult. I can speak from the perspective of several hundred books plus bitter personal experience. God has been able to turn even this great evil into good.

After the Lord had dealt with me on the occult, Bill gave me a copy of Watchman Nee's *Release of the Spirit*. The theme of the book is that the Spirit cannot really be released until both the body and the soul have been broken.

God had brought me to Baltimore to break me, to show me what it meant to die out to my self. In Montana, I had had a beautiful million-dollar church, a parochial school, and a radio program. St. John was a prestigious church in Libby. In Baltimore, I had a little black congregation in a glorified storefront in the heart of the ghetto. I sat in Babylon and remembered Jerusalem. How could I sing the Lord's song in a strange land?

We had plans to build a new church, but they fell through. We tried to buy another church, but the prices were always too high. The racial problem in Baltimore proved far worse than I had anticipated. St. Mark's in Brooklyn was integrated in 1956, but in Baltimore it wasn't even 1950 yet on the racial calendar, and the constant tension was depressing.

I didn't know it yet, but the Lord was breaking me. He was breaking my pride, self-confidence, and self-importance. He was taking away my reliance on my own intelligence and experience. We went into debt for the first time; He was also taking away my financial security. Before the Spirit can be released, everything of the old creation, everything that is not of God, must be stripped away and broken. "Unless a grain of wheat falls into the ground and dies, it remains alone; but if it dies, it bears much fruit."

In August, I finished my program at Lutheran Hospital and went to the first Lutheran Charismatic Conference at Minneapolis. Some nine thousand people were gathered there, most of them Lutherans. They had come to celebrate the renewal of the church. I remembered eight years before when I was alone. What a mighty host the Lord had called up in so short a time. The year before in St. Louis, some two hundred pastors met at the seminary. We knew that something was happening, but no one dreamed that it would move this fast.

Early in September of 1972, my phone rang. It was the president of a nearby Lutheran church. He had read an article I wrote in a local Lutheran newspaper and wanted to discuss the possibility of his church merging with mine.

When I had first come to Baltimore, I had to buy a house, since St. Matthew had no parsonage. Moreover, I had to make the decision quickly since my family and furniture were on the way. The house I decided on was large and well built. It seemed to be a good buy, although it was located in the city in an integrated neighborhood near the slums. My family complained about the neighborhood numerous times, and after Margie was mugged outside our garage, I began to have serious doubts about the wisdom of my choice. Why did I buy this particular house? Was the Lord really guiding me when I made the choice? Now the question was being answered. The church that wanted to merge with St. Matthew was located right across the street.

Our Saviour was a Lutheran church of the same synod as St. Matthew. It was still predominantly white, even though its neighborhood had been changing for about ten years. In the past few years, it had been in decline, with most of its members commuting from some distance away. The average age of the congregation was about sixty, and in spite of valiant efforts by both pastor and people, it had not been able to adequately reach the neighborhood.

At the same time, the Northwood section of Baltimore in which the church was located had a tremendous religious vacuum. Over thirty thousand black people lived in this area, but there was not one significant black church and very few white churches which had gotten past the stage of token integration.

The proposed merger between St. Matthew and Our Saviour proposed instant integration on a totally equal basis with a bi-racial approach to the community. Our Saviour had the image of a white church and that needed to be changed if black people in the neighborhood were to be reached in significant numbers.

When the discussions began, I deliberately kept my hands off, because I felt strongly that this was of the Lord, and I didn't want to hinder in any way. Our Saviour had a beautiful plant that could not be replaced today for less than two million dollars. St. Matthew could offer only a few black Lutheran faces and a slightly worn inner-city pastor.

St. Matthew was in full agreement with the proposal— with certain reservations about its loss of identity. Certain people in Our Saviour were understandably reluctant to invite a black congregation to join them. Other people had reservations about me. We decided that I had to be exposed to the people of Our Saviour. After a few meetings, the attitudes began to change. It was plain that God's hand was in this venture. I was simply standing by, watching what He was doing. Whatever He had in mind, we knew it was going to be wonderful.

For forty years the little black Lutheran church of St. Matthew had been in temporary quarters in the ghetto. They had tried to build, and they had tried to buy, but nothing ever quite seemed to work out. Pastors and lay people worked very hard, and many gave their lives for the dream of St. Matthew. Now suddenly the Lord was offering them a magnificent house of worship in one of the most strategic spots in the city. This was no doubt the greatest challenge in their whole history. They all felt a little anxious, but knew that this was God's plan. "Not by might, not by power, but by my spirit says the Lord."

In January of 1973, the merger was passed. In February, I was called as co-pastor of the newly merged congregations effective April first. It was agreed that St. Matthew would sell its old church and buy my home as a parsonage for the new Our Saviour. The combined rosters of the new church included almost eight hundred baptized members, black and white. Suddenly we had a beautiful building located in a very strategic spot with a large parsonage right across the street. We had no debts and money in the bank. All at one stroke we had a new church, an integrated congregation, plus an almost unlimited challenge. All I had done was to pray.

Everything that the Lord had taken away, He had given back tenfold. At the age of fifty-six, I faced the biggest job of my entire life. I felt humble, a little frightened, and almost overwhelmed with gratitude and praise. Truly God does all things well! He has set before us an open door which no man can shut. As I finish this, we are preparing to celebrate God's new creation on Sunday, April 1. We fervently pray and ask you the reader to join us, that our venture of faith may set a pattern for Lutheran integration. The Spirit is able to break down all barriers.

AUTHOR'S NOTE

The Gift Is Already Yours was originally released in 1973. In 1978 full rights reverted to the author, and this edition is being published by Bethany Fellowship in Minneapolis.

Outside of a few minor corrections, I have decided to leave the story as is, adding only this update. Hundreds of people have said to me since the book was first released, "The story isn't finished. What about the rest?" No Christian story is ever finished, because life is growth and eternal life is no exception.

The Gift Is Already Yours is a witness book. It represents an elemental, sometimes ecstatic, state of spiritual awakening. I would not retract a word of it, but now the waters run deeper and quieter as the stream of life winds nearer home. Sometimes I wonder if it would not have been better to tell no man about the Baptism in the Spirit. Did God really intend that there be a charismatic renewal at all? Or did He perhaps want to renew His Church by quietly and deeply renewing the hearts of His people? The labels, the cultural baggage, the anti-rationalism and the endless controversies would not seem to fit the profile of the Spirit. I know many "Closet Charismatics" whom the Lord has abundantly blessed, yet I have never been openly persecuted for being charismatic. In fact, the label has been profitable in many ways. At the same time, I feel a need to dissociate myself from some things that have been happening under this label.

Often at a renewal gathering I have the feeling that I am seeing the same movie over and over again. Sometimes in counseling I see people who have seemingly been decompensated by the Spirit. Everything was fine until the Spirit came, but nothing has gone right since. Sometimes I have the feeling that there are actually two separate charismatic renewals: one based on the law and the other on the gospel. Law-oriented renewal is just as frightening as any other religion of law. The Gospel is always gospel no matter where it is found.

I say all this not to be critical but to be honest and believable. We need to share the good news and the bad news; otherwise, no one who is authentically human can identify with our testimony.

Recently a group of Missouri Synod Lutheran pastors in St. Paul told me their horror stories about charismatics. I said, "I know, I could tell you many more, but I also know the basis for your concern. I know you are hurting, because I have been there too. The issue is not charismatics or spiritual gifts at all; it's something entirely different. It's called flesh. I don't care what label you put on the spiritual experience I now enjoy. I would never go back to what I was before. Every Sunday morning 2,300 people put their arms around me. That's good and I want to stay there if I can. Call it love, call it gospel, call it charismatic, call it fanatic; it's the way the church ought to feel."

I cannot always identify with everything that happens at North Heights Lutheran Church. Sometimes the preaching, the teaching, and the worship leave something to be desired, but I know it's the body of Christ, because I can feel it. To be surrounded by people who love the Lord and each other and who believe that God is real is an experience that can never be faked. That is what charismatic renewal is all about. At the same time, I believe that we need to move on, to mature and bear fruit.

When the world looks at the average congregation quarreling over trivia, it must marvel and say, "See how they hate one another." Too often standard religion is nothing more than a collection of prejudices. There are indeed abuses in charismatic renewal. They reflect in part the cultural baggage of the classical Pentecostal and Holiness movements. But even more, they reflect the uncertain sound of ecclesiastical leadership. Sometimes the wrong people are feeding and leading, but all too often the hungry sheep are feeding and leading themselves. Whatever the abberations of the confused charismatic may be, they are to be preferred to the death rattle of a moribund church. Warts and all, the church is still the Body of Christ. The time for coming out is past; it's a time to go back in and renew.

EPILOGUE

The epilogue really begins on Christmas Day 1971 when Dr. Bill Backus in Minneapolis received a prophecy. He wrote, "I was in the spirit on Christmas Day when the Lord spoke to me about you." In the past fifteen years I have heard thousands of prophecies. Many of them were so general in nature that they could apply to almost anything. Many others simply did not come true.

This prophecy was different. It was biblical, specific and painfully clear. The prophet also was different, a clinical psychologist-theologian who had been walking in the Spirit only seven months. He was not the kind of man who would easily confuse personal whimsey with divine revelation.

> O priest of God, come up out of captivity in Babylon and go to Jerusalem (Ezra 2) and learn to apply yourself to good deeds, so as to help cases of urgent need, and not to be unfruitful (Titus 3:14). Trust in the Lord; and through the steadfast love of the Most High, you shall not be moved (Psalm 21:7). I stretched out my hand against you because you played the harlot (Ezekiel 16), but you have received of my hand double for all your sins, and your warfare is over (Isaiah 40).

But what was Babylon and where was Jerusalem? Was Babylon the ghetto from which I was finally to be released? I had no problem identifying Brooklyn or Baltimore with Babylon. New York had some redeeming features, but the sky hung low over Baltimore. Although

146

the surroundings were extraordinarily beautiful, Baltimore always depressed me for reasons I could never fully understand. Was the command, "Go back to the city and die," spoken at the foot of a mountain in Guatemala and Montana, now rescinded? Did "playing the harlot" refer to my dabbling in the occult?

The prophecy was put on the shelf until 1974 in Seattle, Washington. I was talking to an Ecumenical group of charismatic pastors about the hardships of ghetto ministry.

"Erve, why did you stay so long?" someone asked. Another said, "You must have loved it. What about your family? How do they feel about living under those conditions?" The questioners kept on prodding.

"No, I didn't really love it. Sometimes all of us hated it very much. Like everybody else, we lusted after suburbia—crabgrass and all."

"Then why did you stay?" several of the brethren asked almost in chorus.

"Because God wanted me to die to self." This is what I told myself. The unconscious tape played constantly.

What did "go back to the city and die" really mean? What does "dying to self" mean literally? As Watchman Nee points out, crucifixion is one form of suicide that is impossible.

On the way to Baltimore from Seattle, I stopped in to see Bill in Minneapolis. He had an entirely different view.

"It's your self-talk, Erve. You've been telling yourself so long that God wants you to suffer that you cannot allow God to bless you. Come down from the cross. It may be just your own. Nowhere in the Scriptures does it say that we are to be constantly stripped, crushed,

147

and tortured. Try saying to yourself, 'God wants to bless and prosper me. He wants me to be happy.' Your self-talk is full of misbeliefs. Just try saying to yourself, 'God loves me.' That's gospel."

"Okay, I'll try saying that. It may not mean anything, but it can't hurt either." I flew back to Baltimore with a new thought planted in my half-closed mind. Had I been brainwashed by Missouri Synod or Pentecostal legalism, or was it merely my own brand?

Sometime later I read in Francis McNutt's book on healing that the cross couldn't be sickness, demons, chronic illness, poverty, hunger, guilt or pain because while Christ was saying, "Take up your cross daily and follow me," He was healing the sick, casting out demons, and feeding the hungry. Charismatics are often accused of living a theology of glory, but was mine really a theology of the cross? Did charismatic "blood theology" mean that we have to bleed all the time? Could a Christian ever be really happy on this sin-cursed earth?

First, the Lord speaks in the still, small voice. He waits for us to listen and to obey. But sometimes He has to get our attention with fire and earthquakes. I was willing to leave Babylon, but first I had to have a call to Jerusalem, wherever that might be. There were no calls and I was afraid to take a leap of pure blind faith. When you are fifty-five years old with four dependent children, you don't just fly off into the wild blue yonder looking for some kind of mystical Jerusalem. How could I really be sure of the Lord's will for me?

There were some leads. I had spent nearly twelve years part time in New York preparing to be a pastoral counselor. Bill wanted me to come to Minneapolis and go into private practice in his clinic, but I just couldn't see the Twin Cities as Jerusalem. Wasn't St. Paul called "the occult capital of the world"? Wasn't Minneapolis a center for Satan worship?

"How about Forest Lake, where I live? Couldn't that be Jerusalem?" Bill would ask.

"It could be if there weren't quite so many mosquitoes," I would quip. Later on I learned that the mosquito is the state bird of Minnesota. "Besides, Jerusalem is a city built on a hill, not in a swamp like Forest Lake." Somehow I couldn't picture Jerusalem under two feet of snow.

When the Jews refused to go to Jerusalem because they were too comfortable among the fleshpots of Europe, the Lord sent fishers and hunters to bring them home (Jer. 16:16). The fishers were the Zionists who tried in vain to coax them. When they failed, the Lord sent the Nazi hunters to smoke them out. The holocaust was the price of the Jewish state founded in 1948. Who can resist His will? Bill was the fisher, but the hunters were still to come.

The Alameda in Baltimore wasn't exactly suburbia, but it was home. Two blocks away on the corner of the Alameda and 33rd Street stood Our Saviour Lutheran Church, looking like a misplaced medieval castle set down in the heart of a crumbling urban ghetto. In 1974 I had become the head pastor. Our Saviour might have looked irrelevant, but it was paid for and had substantial financial resources besides. Its program of integration wasn't popular in north Baltimore, but it was security.

Our home on the Alameda was only two blocks from Memorial Stadium. Whenever the Baltimore Orioles or the Colts played a home game, we had up to sixty-seven thousand guests practically in our front yard. But our home was also a fortress. The walls were a foot thick, the floors hardwood, the walk-in closets lined with cedar, and the slate shingles almost an inch thick. There were eight bedrooms, three full baths, and a three-car garage. When we closed the triple storm windows, Memorial Stadium, the ghettos and the world were shut out. The house was purchased in 1971 for thirty thousand dollars. Today it would bring in at least three times that amount. It was a bargain, because few middle-class white families wanted to live in a black neighborhood. But how could I be the pastor of an integrated church unless I lived in an integrated neighborhood?

When we moved into it in 1971, the neighborhood was changing rapidly. By 1975 it had become almost 90 percent black. The lower end of the Alameda had also become a jungle. The first two years were relatively quiet even though Margie was initiated to the area by being mugged at our back door in broad daylight. But in 1975 we seemed to lose our covering entirely. In less than a year there were a dozen serious incidents involving firearms. I didn't rise to the fishers' bait; had the hunters now arrived? Was the Lord trying to tell me something by putting us under a state of virtual siege? Was the "Babylonian captivity" of the Pranges about to come to an abrupt and forced end?

The first hunter came at five o'clock on Sunday morning. In the twilight zone between dream and waking fantasy, I heard my eighteen-year-old son yelling, "If you don't stop, I'm going to blow your head off!" He was holding a 38 revolver against the face of a young drug addict who insisted on breaking into the house.

The second hunter came the next Sunday morning— also at 5:00 a.m. This time I was awakened by my twenty-one-year-old daughter screaming from one of the upstairs bedrooms, "There's someone in my room!"

My son ran upstairs with a handgun and found a young man hanging by his fingers on the balcony door. When Mark approached him with the gun, the intruder leaped some sixteen feet to the ground and fled into the morning darkness.

There were night hunters, too. When my daughters came home at 2:00 a.m. after working as waitresses in a downtown Italian restaurant, men would be sitting in parked cars waiting for them. We had to take turns riding shotgun to escort them from the garage to the house. Once Margie looked out the window to see if the rapists were waiting—right into the eyeballs of a Peeping Tom with his face pressed against the glass.

The police were somewhat less than helpful. According to their understanding, it was necessary for them to catch the criminal in the act. Statistically, this happened about once in a hundred times, and then the intruder stood one chance in a hundred of going to jail. The odds were definitely in favor of the criminal. One candid cop said to me, "Rev, don't depend on us; we've got all we can do just keeping ourselves alive. Just don't shoot anybody, because then you will be the burglar and the odds won't be a hundred to one in your favor."

We got the message and moved—not to Jerusalem, but to Joppatown, which was right next to Jerusalem on the Chesapeake Bay. The hunters had one last parting shot. The furniture was all moved and the children were already in Joppatown. Margie and I were sleeping downstairs on a mattress prior to loading up the last items. Sampson, the Siberian Husky who couldn't bark, was with us. Suddenly in the middle of the night someone broke in upstairs. We could hear the footsteps of two men above our heads. But there was nothing left upstairs, so they started down the stairs. Quickly I grabbed a gun and waited at the bottom doorway. I assumed they were armed, and I wasn't going to let them fire the first shot. The telephone was already disconnected. Margie waited quietly behind me in the dining room.

The gun I held in my hand was a 357 magnum, one of the most powerful handguns that could be purchased. I knew how to use it. Somebody was going to die. In five years of war I had never killed a man. I could see the headlines: "Pastor shoots burglars in empty house." The doorknob turned slowly. I pulled back the hammer on the gun and aimed where I thought a man's body would appear.

My finger pressed against the trigger. My watch was ticking, "Thou shalt not kill; thou shalt not kill." Every beat of my heart seemed to be saying, "Murderer, murderer." The westerns and cop shows were right after all. The first man you kill is the hardest. Some people never get over it, while others never can break the habit.

"Lord, do you want Margie and me to be killed instead of these burglars? Whose life is more valuable? But on second thought, don't answer that."

For the first time in his life Sampson barked. It sounded more like the roar of a lion in that empty house. Burglars are more afraid of dogs than of guns. Sampson weighed almost 80 pounds, but he sounded twice that big. Like a flash the intruders ran up the stairs, leaped off the balcony, and disappeared into the night. It seemed like an eternity, but it had lasted only three minutes—three minutes of eternity. My hands, still innocent of human

152

blood, were now shaking tremulously. "I got your message, Lord; we're moving."

Sampson was a beautiful Siberian Husky. He was a lousy watchdog, but no one knew that because he was so big. He just wanted to be loved, but his overtures of friendship were all too often misunderstood. When he slept in the picture window of our rented house in Joppatown, his very presence was a warning. Ours was almost the only house on the block not broken into. In fact, we had few intrusions from salesmen or canvassers. It is somewhat disconcerting to ring a doorbell and then stare right into the eyeballs of a dog six-feet tall on his hind legs. It's even more intimidating when the dog looks like a wolf, has one blue and one brown eye, and howls instead of barking. One day I came home and found a mangled shirt, a pair of torn trousers and several Watch Tower tracts on the front steps. I cornered Sampson, stared first in his brown eye and then in his blue eye and asked pointedly, "Sampson, tell me the truth. Did you or did not eat a Jehovah's Witness?" His tail wagged and he looked terribly guilty, but to this day the question remains unanswered. Now he is dead and I may never know.

It's difficult for me to write about Trinity Lutheran Church in Joppatown. In a way it was both a wonderful and tragic experience. There were so many tremendous people there. Perhaps I will know someday what my role really was. Perhaps it was only a stopover on the way to Jerusalem. But it was a spiritual watergate. My discernment seemed to have gone blind for a time. As a friend put it later, "When the Lord wants Daniel to go into the lions' den, He doesn't tell him in advance, or else he won't go."

153

In June of 1976 the Lord spoke plainly, "Go." At the same time I received notice of a pastoral call from North Heights Lutheran Church in St. Paul, Minnesota. I was to be the associate pastor for counseling at North Heights half time, and also to go into counseling practice with Dr. Backus in his psychological clinic. How beautifully the Lord had arranged everything. At least so we thought.

On the last day of July, 1976, Margie and I drove from Baltimore to the Twin Cities. We were going to take in the International Lutheran Conference on the Holy Spirit and also find a house. After the conference was over, Margie would return to Joppatown and move the furniture and family to our new home in the Twin Cities, or was it Jerusalem?

We arrived at the Curtis Hotel in Minneapolis on Saturday evening, August 1. I parked the car in the Curtis Hotel garage, carried the bags up to our room, and prepared to relax before the conference opened on the next day. But there was to be no relaxing for many days. There was a notice on the door saying that Baltimore had been trying frantically to reach us all day. I picked up the telephone with deep foreboding and called the number. Mark had been involved in an auto accident in Joppatown. He was lying near death in the trauma section of University Hospital in downtown Baltimore.

We called our daughter Diane in Joppatown. She said that Mark had been a passenger in an auto involved in a head-on collision. The combined impact speed was almost 130 miles per hour. He had put on a seat belt just twenty seconds before the crash, and the seat belt had almost cut him in two. We called the trauma section directly. Mark was conscious. I talked with him and prayed with him over the telephone. All he could say was, "Dad, pray! Pray! Get everybody at the conference to pray!" That was the first time I had known him to be so interested in prayer.

What should we do? Margie and I prayed together for almost two hours. We were united in prayer and tears as we had never been before. The next day Margie flew back to Baltimore, but the Lord told me to stay. I was heavily involved in the conference program. "Minister to my children and I will minister to yours," He seemed to be saying.

On Thursday night I spoke to the conference on the family covenant: "Believe on the Lord Jesus Christ and you will be saved and your household." Over ten thousand people joined together in prayer for Mark. That night the Lord showed me that salvation included far more than just our souls. It also included the healing and protection of our bodies and our families. Once more He emphasized that we are not saved just as individuals but as families.

Mark spent almost a month in the hospital. At one point they took all forty feet of his intestines out and went through them inch by inch. His recovery was full and gratifying. Today he is a straight "A" senior at Bethel College—tall, handsome, and filled with the Spirit. The Lord not only answered our prayers for healing, but also gave us many bonuses for which we had not even asked.

He also blessed the ministry at North Heights and my counseling practice beyond every fantasy that we could possibly have entertained. According to the family covenant, He included every family member in the blessing: Karen, Bill, and granddaughter, Raechel, in Baltimore, plus Diane and Stephen in Minnesota. Diane was accepted into a Ph.D. program at the University of Minnesota and was also made director of marketing of U.S. Financial Services. Stephen suddenly grew up and became an "A" student at Bethel College. My cup runneth over.

But what about Jerusalem? Did we ever locate it? Two years ago the Lord began to build us a house. First, He chose ten wooded acres in Forest Lake and then built a beautiful five-bedroom house, off the road in the middle of the woods. It's so quiet you can almost hear the mosquitoes brushing their teeth. The deer, the pheasants, and the squirrels quietly walk past the back door—even the snow apologizes for intruding. We never had to live in the suburbia I had so often reacted against. We went straight from the city to the forest.

This is the word that the Lord gave and placed upon the doorpost:

> Upon your walls, O Jerusalem, I have set watchmen; all the day and all the night they shall never be silent. You who put the Lord in remembrance, take no rest, and give him no rest until he establishes Jerusalem and makes it a praise in the earth. The Lord has sworn by his right hand and by his mighty arm. (Isa. 62:6-8, RSV).

It was not the cities or Forest Lake, but our place that was Jerusalem!

We moved into Jerusalem, just up the road from Bill's house, in September of '77. Shortly afterwards Bill had one more word from the Lord:

> But be glad and rejoice for ever in that which I create; for behold, I create Jerusalem a rejoicing, and her people a joy. I will rejoice in Jerusalem, and be glad in my people; no more shall be heard in it the sound of weeping and the cry of distress. No more shall there be in it an infant that lives but a few days, or an

old man who does not fill out his days, for the child shall die a hundred years old, and the sinner a hundred years old shall be accursed. They shall build houses and inhabit them; they shall plant vineyards and eat their fruit. They shall not build and another inhabit; they shall not plant and another eat; for like the days of a tree shall the days of my people be, and my chosen shall long enjoy the work of their hands. They shall not labor in vain, or bear children for calamity; for they shall be the offspring of the blessed of the Lord, and their children with them. Before they call I will answer, while they are yet speaking I will hear. The wolf and the lamb shall feed together, and the lion shall eat straw like the ox; and dust shall be the serpent's food. They shall not hurt or destroy in all my holy mountain. (Isa. 65:18-25, RSV)

Everything seemed to fit. But where was the wolf? Shortly before we moved in, Sampson went to the heavenly Jerusalem when a neighbor mistook him for a wolf. We were still in mourning when Barbara Rynders called us about an ad in the paper. It said simply, "Arctic wolf for sale, one-quarter Husky," and so Simon came into our lives, pure white and pure love. He stayed long enough to make a lie of every story about the savage ferocity of wolves—then suddenly he was gone. We mourned for almost eight months and then unexpectedly he was back—bigger, whiter, and more loving than ever. Was I imagining or were there really folded wings underneath that thick ruff on his neck and shoulders? Although his jaws could crush with the force of fifteen hundred pounds, a child could take a bone away from him without danger. Was this a living promise of the new Jerusalem?

The following spring I planted a thousand trees. When

they mature I shall be a hundred and thirty, but who cares. Our Jerusalem is a timeless place. The angels of the trees and of the wind breathe their daily benediction above it. It is an Eden where we have taken authority over the elemental spirits of the universe, so that the mosquitoes scarcely dare to bite. Heaven and earth touch whenever God is present and real, and the whole creation waits with bated breath for yet further unveiling of His glorious will.

In 1977 I chose early and honorable retirement from the Lutheran Church—Missouri Synod. This has set me free to minister to all Lutherans. For over two years I have conducted a healing, deliverance and counseling ministry at North Heights. This has also included preaching and teaching. The Lord has blessed the ministry beyond any expectations. Sometimes people from five different states come to our altar in a single day. The counseling practice in Dr. Backus' clinic has allowed me to wipe out the debts incurred during the ghetto years (and, as Margie says, make new and bigger ones). For the first time in twenty-six years we have a real home. I spend five days a week at the church and the clinic ministering to cases of urgent need. Two days a week are spent at home in Jerusalem writing. The time for experiencing and taking in is about past. Now is the time for writing it all down.

BIBLIOGRAPHY

Barclay, William. *The Apostles' Creed for Everyman*. New York: Harper and Row, 1967.

Barclay, William. *The Beatitudes and the Lord's Prayer for Everyman*. New York: Harper and Row, 1968.

Bennett, Dennis J. *Nine O'Clock in the Morning*. Plainfield, New Jersey: Logos International, 1970.

Blumhardt, Christoph. *Die Heilung Von Kranken Durch Glaubensgebet*. Germany: Volksdienst Verlag, Leipzig, 1924.

Blumhardt, Christoph. *Evening Prayers*. Rifton, New York: Plough Publishing House, 1972.

Bonhoeffer, Dietrich. *The Cost of Discipleship*. New York: The MacMillan Company, 1960.

Buttrick, George Arthur. *God, Pain and Evil*. New York: Abingdon Press, 1966.

Buttrick, George Arthur. *Prayer*. New York: Abingdon Press, 1952.

Christenson, Laurence. *Speaking in Tongues*. Minneapolis, Minnesota: Bethany Fellowship, 1968.

Cruz, Nicky (with Jamie Buckingham). *Run Baby Run*. Plainfield, New Jersey: Logos International, 1968.

Frost, Robert C. *Aglow with the Spirit*. Plainfield, New Jersey: Logos International, 1971.

Harkness, Georgia. *The Fellowship of the Holy Spirit*. New York: Abingdon Press, 1966.

Heiler, Friedrich. *Prayer*. New York: Oxford University Press, 1958.

Heim, Karl. *Christian Faith and Natural Science*. New

York: Harper and Brothers, 1953.

Heinecken, Martin J. *The Moment Before God.* Philadelphia: Muhlenberg Press, 1956.

James, William. *The Varieties of Religious Experience.* New York: Random House, 1902.

Kelsey, Morton T. *Tongue Speaking.* Garden City, New York: Doubleday and Company, Incorporated, 1964.

Kierkegaard, Soren. *Works of Love.* Princeton, New Jersey: Princeton University Press, 1949.

Kittel, Gerhard, ed. *Theological Dictionary of the New Testament.* 8 Volumes. Grand Rapids, Michigan: William B. Eerdmans Publishing Company, 1964.

Koenig, Richard Edwin. *If God Is God.* St. Louis, Missouri: Concordia Publishing House, 1969.

Laubach, Frank C. *Prayer, the Mightiest Force in the World.* Old Tappan, New Jersey: Fleming H. Revell Company, 1946.

Laubach, Frank C. *War of Amazing Love.* Westwood, New Jersey: Fleming H. Revell Company, 1965.

Lewis, C. S. *A Mind Awake.* New York: Harcourt, Brace & World, Inc., 1969.

Lewis, C. S. *The Four Loves.* New York: Harcourt, Brace and Company, 1960.

Lewis, C. S. *The Great Divorce.* New York: The MacMillan Company, 1964.

Lewis, C. S. *The Screwtape Letters.* New York: MacMillan, 1948.

Nee, Watchman, *The Ministry of God's Word.* New York: Christian Fellowship Publications, Incorporated, 1971.

Nee, Watchman. *The Normal Christian Worker.* Hong Kong: Hong Kong Church Book Room, 1965.

Nee, Watchman. *The Release of the Spirit.* Cloverdale, Indiana: Sure Foundation Publication, 1965.

Nee, Watchman. *Spiritual Authority*. New York: Christian Fellowship Publications, Incorporated, 1971.

Nee, Watchman. *The Spiritual Man*. New York: Christian Fellowship Publications, Incorporated, 1969.

Nee, Watchman. *A Table in the Wilderness*. Fort Washington, Pennsylvania: Christian Literature Crusade, 1969.

Nygren, Anders. *Agape and Eros*. Philadelphia: The Westminister Press, 1953.

O'Connor, Edward D. *The Pentecostal Movement in the Catholic Church*. Notre Dame, Indiana: Ave Maria Press, 1971.

Prenter, Regin. *Spiritus Creator*. Philadelphia: Fortress Press, 1953.

Pulkingham, W. Graham. *Gathered for Power*. New York: Morehouse-Barlow Company, 1972.

Sanford, Agnes. *Behold Your God*. St. Paul, Minnesota: Macalester Park Publishing Company, 1958.

Sanford, Agnes. *The Healing Power of the Bible*. New York: J. B. Lippincott Company, 1966.

Sayers, Dorothy L. *The Man Born To Be King*. Grand Rapids, Michigan: William B. Eerdmans Publishing Company, 1943.

Schlink, Basilea. *Ruled by the Spirit*. Minneapolis, Minnesota: Bethany Fellowship, Inc., Dimension Books, 1970.

Sherrill, John L. *They Speak with Other Tongues*. Westwood, New Jersey: Fleming H. Revell Company, 1965.

Shoemaker, Sam. *Extraordinary Living for Ordinary Men*. Grand Rapids, Michigan: Zondervan Publishing House, 1965.

Smith, Timothy L. *Called Unto Holiness*. Kansas City,

Missouri: Nazarene Publishing House, 1962.

Stewart, James S. *The Gates of New Life*. New York: Charles Scribner's Sons, 1940.

Stewart, James S. *The Wind of the Spirit*. New York: Abingdon Press, 1968.

Strommen, Merton P.; Brekke, Milo L.; Underwager, Ralph C.; and Johnson, Arthur L. *A Study of Generations*. Minneapolis, Minnesota: Augsburg Publishing House, 1972.

Tari, Mel. *Like a Mighty Wind*. Carol Stream, Illinois: Creation House, 1971.

Thielicke, Helmut. *Between God and Satan*. Grand Rapids, Michigan: William B. Eerdmans Publishing Company, 1958.

Thielicke, Helmut. *I Believe—The Christian's Creed*. Philadelphia: Fortress Press, 1968.

Thielicke, Helmut. *Life Can Begin Again*. Philadelphia: Fortress Press, 1963.

Thielicke, Helmut. *Our Heavenly Father*. New York: Harper and Brothers, 1960.

Thielicke, Helmut. *Out of the Depths*. Grand Rapids, Michigan: William B. Eerdmans Publishing Company, 1962.

Thielicke, Helmut. *The Silence of God*. Grand Rapids, Michigan: William B. Eerdmans Publishing Company, 1962.

Thielicke, Helmut. *The Waiting Father*. New York: Harper and Row, 1959.

Tournier, Paul. *The Adventure of Living*. New York: Harper and Row, 1963.

Tournier, Paul. *A Doctor's Casebook in the Light of the Bible*. New York: Harper and Row, 1960.

Tournier, Paul. *Guilt and Grace*. New York: Harper and Row, 1962.

Tournier, Paul. *A Place for You*. New York: Harper and Row, 1966.

Tournier, Paul. *The Strong and the Weak*. Philadelphia: The Westminster Press, 1963.

Trueblood, Elton. *The Incendiary Fellowship*. New York: Harper and Row, 1967.

Underhill, Evelyn. *Mysticism*. New York: Meridan Books, 1955.

Wallis, Arthur. *Pray in the Spirit*. Fort Washington, Pennsylvania: Christian Literature Crusade, 1970.

Weatherhead, Leslie D. *That Immortal Sea*. New York: Abingdon Press, 1953.

White, Anne S. *Dayspring*. Plainfield, New Jersey: Logos International, 1971.

Wingren, Gustaf. *The Living Word*. Philadelphia: Fortress Press, 1960.